The Tall Tale in American Folklore ᴀ Literature

The Tall Tale
in American Folklore and Literature

Carolyn S. Brown

THE UNIVERSITY OF TENNESSEE PRESS / KNOXVILLE

Copyright © 1987 by The University of Tennessee Press / Knoxville.
All Rights Reserved. Manufactured in the United States of America.
Cloth: 1st printing, 1987; 2nd printing, 1988; 3rd printing, 1989.
Paper: 1st printing, 1989.

The paper in this book meets the minimum requirements of the
American National Standard for Permanence of Paper for Printed
Library Materials. ∞ The binding materials have been chosen
for strength and durability.

Library of Congress Cataloging-in-Publication Data

Brown, Carolyn S. (Carolyn Schmidt)
    The tall tale in American folklore and literature.

    Bibliography: p.
    Includes index.
    1. Tall tales — United States — History and criticism
2. American wit and humor — History and criticism.
3. American literature — 19th century — History and
criticism.   4. Literature and folklore — United States.
5 Folklore in literature   6. Folklore — United States.
I. Title
PS437.B76   1987   813.'009   86–25125
ISBN 0–87049–529–1 (cloth: alk. paper)
ISBN 0–87049–627–1 (pbk.: alk. paper)

For Yorke

Preface

The study of folklore in literature was for years dominated by source hunters in search of specific plots, motifs, or beliefs adapted or incorporated from folklore into fiction or poetry. This preoccupation with data, among scholars of folklore in literature, paralleled folklorists' own emphasis on tale cataloging and motif tracing during the heyday of the Finnish historic-geographic method of folktale study. In the early 1960s a revolution occurred among folklorists, inspired by Dell Hymes and others studying the ethography of speaking.[1] To the new generation of folklorists, the text of a folktale comprises only one aspect of a complex storytelling event. To them, "the telling is the tale"[2]: not simply the plot or motif, but the plot as told by a particular narrator to a particular audience on a particular occasion.

If "the telling is the tale" in folklore, then the study of folktales in literature should also go beyond motif tracing and source hunting and consider how that complex interaction between tale, teller, and audience has been transferred to print. And so there have arisen new approaches to the study of folklore in literature. Some folklorist-critics attempt a deeper analysis of the meanings and functions of the folklore that appears in literature, and of the writer's motives for putting it there. In doing so the critics uncover new layers of meaning in the literary text.[3] Others, following the lead of Roger Abrahams, stress the communicative aspects of both folklore and literature. To Abrahams, art is performance, and performance is a two-sided interaction between artist and audience. While these folklorists have been developing performance theory, modern literary critics have become increasingly interested in reader response.[4] Out of these two parallel developments, a new method of studying folklore in literature is evolving. According to Sandra Stahl, "It is when both folklore and literature are regarded as performances involving artists and audiences that the two fields that study such 'performances' seem most effectively allied."[5]

My own contribution to this growing field of study centers on the idea of a folktale genre as a specific mode of performance which can be adapted and translated into literature. A genre, as opposed to a tale type, is distinguished by the kind of material presented, by the function it serves in the community, and by the rhetorical relationship between artist and audience. If I am interested in the use of tall tales in nineteenth-century American literature, I will want first to understand the tall tale as an oral genre, and only then to examine its specific appearances in individual literary works. I will concern myself very little with a writer's specific oral sources and will concentrate on his manipulation of the tall tale genre. I will want, especially, to compare the writer's mode of communicating and interpreting tallness with the folk yarnspinner's methods and motives for telling tall tales.

This approach to tall tales results in a somewhat bifurcated work which concentrates on different, though parallel, subjects in each of two distinct parts: the tall tale in folklore and the tall tale in literature. In the first chapter, I survey the historical interactions between folktale and literary tale in America that make this joint treatment possible and necessary. In Chapter II, I concentrate on the folklore, defining and describing the tall tale as an oral genre with its own peculiar techniques, its own aesthetic, and its own cultural functions. With this theoretical background established, I turn to the literature. Chapter III is entitled "Flush Times," for the antebellum period when the oral tale's tremendous popularity spilled over into a great flood of popular humorous writing. Chapter IV presents a tall tale reading of George Washington Harris' raucous, controversial *Sut Lovingood*. Chapter V looks at Mark Twain's discovery of a tall tale style, character, and attitude in *Roughing It;* and Chapter VI examines his taller-than-life *Autobiography*. Chapter VII, primarily using material from Mark Twain, briefly demonstrates the tall tale's influence on American prose style even when no dialect-speaking tall yarnspinner is in sight. Finally, the epilogue offers a glance at the modern children and grandchildren of the nineteenth-century literary tall tale.

Ultimately, the bifurcation between the folklore section and the remaining chapters is more apparent than real. I adhere throughout to the principle that a clear understanding of the oral and written tall tale can best be achieved when the two forms are studied together and the skills and techniques of two disciplines are brought to bear on each. The written tall tale should, of course, be handled with the tools of literary criticism, but it imitates and reflects a vigorous oral tradition that must be approached through the methods of folklore research. On the other hand, our understanding of the oral tall tale can be enriched if we approach it not only as folk tradition and communication, but also as a work of art created by a particular artist. And so in the end our bifurcated vision is really a stereoscopic vision that, by showing two different images of the tall tale, gives a more complete picture than one image alone could ever achieve.

This study was begun as a dissertation at the University of Virginia. I wish to thank the faculty and my fellow graduate students there for helping me achieve the scholarly and intellectual foundation that then enabled me to finish the work far from Charlottesville. I am especially grateful to Professors Harold Kolb and Charles Perdue for helping me to conceive this project in the first place and then for providing essential advice, criticism, and encouragement through the many years until its completion. In the final stages, Milton Rickels and Daniel Barnes provided critical readings for which I am very grateful. Lastly, I wish to thank my husband, Yorke, for his untiring support, his inspiring example, and his inexhaustible confidence in me.

Contents

Illustrations

The Tall Tale in American Folklore and Literature

CHAPTER 1

Inseparable Strands:
The Intertwining of Oral and Printed Yarns

"I swallowed it jest as he gin it to me!" shouted the Sucker.
—"Swallowing an Oyster Alive, a Story of Illinois
— by a Missourian"

Near the Peaks of Otter on Virginia's Blue Ridge, the Baptist church operates a boys' summer camp that covers 510 acres of woodland surrounded by national forest and national park lands. One Monday afternoon in midsummer, as a new group of campers arrived for their week's stay, a nervous mother spoke to the camp director about conditions at the camp. "Do y'all have much trouble with snakes up here?" she asked. "No ma'am, we really don't," the camp director replied soberly. "The mountain lions eat 'em." Once started, the director piled one stretcher on top of another for the joint benefit of this gullible lady and an appreciative forest ranger who listened with a solemn face but a gleam of recognition and delight in his eye.[1]

Don Lewis, the camp director, is no backwoods, tobacco-chewing old-timer. Thirty-some years old, raised in a suburb of Washington, D.C., college and seminary educated, he is, nonetheless, a contemporary tall tale artist who tells his stories to friends and strangers, visiting parents and young campers, colleagues and casual acquaintances. His tales, and his attitude toward them, derive from an oral storytelling tradition that does not discriminate against the twentieth century, education, or the suburbs. As Don Lewis tells it, the tall tale is a comic

fiction disguised as fact, deliberately exaggerated to the limits of credibility or beyond in order to reveal emotional truths, to awaken his audience, to exorcise fears, to define and bind a social group. From all we
know, the nineteenth-century American tall tale was the same. And as
it moved from folklore into subliterature and literature, it often re-
tained its essential characteristics and meanings. The most artistically
successfull tall tale writers were those who most creatively transformed
folklore's subtler functions and meanings into tall literature.

Although it was neither invented in nor restricted to North America, the tall tale has held a place of special significance in American
life. From almost the beginning, the incomprehensible vastness of the
continent, the extraordinary fertility of the land, and the variety of natural peculiarities inspired a humor of extravagance and exaggeration,
while the American's need to affirm the value of a culture in many ways
independent of European refinements, constraints, and mores engen-
dered a humor that was clubby, exclusive. The vast difference among
America's geographic sections, too, gave impetus to comic exaggeration. Thus the tall tale became a tool and an emblem of national and
regional identity.[2]

Europeans and Americans alike have judged the tall tale to be more
peculiarly American than other types of humor. Early visitors to America, as well as those who never crossed the ocean but read the travelers'
accounts or saw imported American plays, agreed that American humor was peculiarly exaggerative.[3] Travelers repeatedly commented on
the American propensity for "swopping stories" as they rode on stagecoaches, steamboats, and railroads, or sat around campfires or in the
town idling places.[4] Most of the stories reported were humorous anecdotes about local characters and American types, and many of them
were quite tall.

As the tall tale flourished on the steamboat and in the barroom, it
also blossomed into popular forms of written humor. The earliest tall
tale writers—the comic playwrights, almanac editors, and newspaper
contributors—found most of their inspiration in the storytelling of the
American people. The theater very early picked up the popular description of a Mississippi backwoodsman as "half a horse and half an alligator"; and a buckskin-clad actor named Noah Ludlow spread the
phrase throughout the Old Southwest in a rousing song about the War
of 1812.[5] The theater also took material from the life and yarns of Mike
Fink, the riverboatman, storyteller, and hellion whose exploits were

known up and down the midwestern rivers. Two years before his death in 1823, some of the tales attached to Fink appeared in Alphonso Wetmore's play *The Peddlar*, and in 1828 Fink first appeared in print in a rather tame gift book account entitled "The Last of the Boatmen." The author, Morgan Neville, claims to have known Fink, and may have heard some of the stories directly from his hero.[6] Stories about Fink later appeared in *The Spirit of the Times, The Western Review,* and several Crockett almanacs. Some of these may have been invented and told by Fink; others were folk tales originally attached to other characters and transferred to Mike Fink either by folk raconteurs or, more likely, by writers who wanted a hero whose name would be familiar to their readers.[7] The Crockett tales have a similar history. Davy Crockett, frontiersman, U.S. senator, and war hero, first told tales about himself and later had tales told and written about him. The Crockett almanacs, published between 1835 and 1856, collected new and old tall motifs.

The flush times of the American literary tall tale fit roughly into the period of 1831 to 1860. The year 1831 saw the first performance of James Kirke Paulding's tall comedy *The Lion of the West* as well as the founding of William Trotter Porter's sporting weekly, *The Spirit of the Times*. During the next few decades, when any itinerant judge or small-time newspaper editor in the Southwest could become a writer of backwoods sketches, tall tales were printed in newspapers, almanacs, and gift books, and were reprinted and circulated throughout the country. They described eccentrics, old-timers, jokers, and hunters who told of huge and clever bears, giant mosquitoes, extraordinary marksmen, and vast deserts and boiling springs of the Far West. Many of these tales appear to be close transcriptions of folktales; others are purely literary inventions imitating folktales, the previously printed versions of American folktales, or the European tall tales collected in R.E. Raspe's *Münchausen*. By the 1850s, tall southwestern fiction was being anthologized not only by Porter and the southern writer T.A. Burke, but also by Thomas Chandler Haliburton, the Nova Scotian who created the comic Yankee Sam Slick and whose six volumes of American humorous writing were published in London as well as Philadelphia.[8] Just as it was settling into a respectable genre—like a frontier becoming civilized— the literary tall tale was disrupted by civil war. In 1861 the suspension of mail service between North and South finished off the already ailing *Spirit*, depriving writers and readers of a major vehicle for tall fiction.[9] During the war years, though oral yarns must still have circulated, in

Don Lewis instructing and entertaining a group of campers at Vanderkamp Center in Cleveland, New York, 1996. Photo by Yorke Press.

literature good-natured humor largely gave way to Patriotic Gore.[10] George Washington Harris, however, stuck with the genre, adapting the tall tale to the changing times by increasing his narrator's virulence as sectional conflict intensified.

After the war, sectional writing was largely taken over by the local colorists, who often sentimentalized folk culture. Still, because the tall tale continued to be told, it continued to appear occasionally in print. Newspaper hoaxes in the Far West attest to its popularity on the newest frontier, as do the works and the testimony of Mark Twain. By the time he reached his maturity, Mark Twain had been strongly influenced both by the storytellers he had lived and worked with and by the Southwest humorists he had read and printed before the war. His major continuations of the tall tale tradition, *Roughing It* and his *Autobiography*, though written after the ebb of the flush times, are the most extended literary uses of the genre by a nineteenth-century writer.

Throughout the century the path of influence between oral and written forms was open in both directions. While the oral tall tale provided inspiration and materials for comic writers, the comedy in popular literature also encouraged the raconteurs. The oral tall tale might never have become so renowned and widespread in America had it not continually been broadcast by the media of popular culture: songs, plays, and newspapers spread the idea of exaggerative humor as well as individual tales. Ludlow's *The Hunters of Kentucky* was performed throughout the Southwest. Writers of tall sketches claimed that the printed yarns directly influenced storytelling sessions. In 1843, a *Spirit* contributor calling himself Major Whetstone reported a storytelling session that included the famous mountaineer Black Harris. Whetstone explains that after he told a tale which had been printed in the "Pikeyoon" the previous spring, Harris told original tales of his hunting and fishing adventures, and ended with a petrified man story. Though this particular exchange of tales may never have occurred, or at least not with Black Harris,[11] there is probably some truth in it. We do know that written tales influence oral tales. Mark Twain, well acquainted with newspaper humor as a printer's devil, in his turn told stories on the steamboats, in the mining camps, and in the newspaper offices. Today Don Lewis and other yarnspinners admit a debt to Mark Twain's writing.

Folklore inspires subliterature; folklore and subliterature inspire literature; and subliterature and literature in turn re-inspire folklore.

Within this complex relationship there is constant changing, shifting; but there is also continuity.

In 1828, James Hall traveled to Illinois and there heard a curious story about deep mud, a gritty native, and an unstoppable horse:

A weary way-farer, who journeyed through Ohio a few years ago, illustrated his remarks upon the badness of the roads, by relating the following *curious fact*. He was floundering through the mire, as many an honest gentleman flounders through life, getting along with difficulty, but still getting along; sometimes wading to the saddle-girth in water, sometimes clambering over logs, and occasionally plunged in a quagmire. While carefully picking his way by a spot more miry than the rest, he espied a man's hat, a very creditable beaver, lying with crown upwards in the mud, and as he approached, was not a little startled to see it *move*. . . . The solitary rider checked his nag, and extending his long whip, fairly upset the hat—when, lo! beneath it appeared a man's head . . . a living laughing head, by which our inquisitive traveller heard himself saluted with "Hullo, stranger! who told you to knock my hat off?" [The traveller apologizes for knocking the hat off and offers to help the man out of the mud.] "Oh, never mind," said the other, "I'm in a rather *bad fix* it is true, but I have an excellent horse under me, who has carried me through many a worse place than this—we shall get along."[12]

Three years later, James Kirke Paulding elaborated the motif in *The Lion of the West*. The play confronts the frontiersman Nimrod Wildfire, modeled after Davy Crockett, with an English lady tourist, modeled after Mrs. Trollope and bent upon recording and reporting the peculiarities of American life.

Wildfire.   The soil—oh, the soil's so rich you may travel under it.

Mrs. Wollope.   Travel under ground, sir? I must put this down.

Wildfire.   Yes, ma'am, particularly after the spring rains. Look you here now, tother day, I was horseback paddling away pretty comfortably through Nobottom swamp, when suddenly—I wish I may be curry-comb'd to death by 50,000 tom cats, if I didn't see a white hat getting along in mighty considerable style all alone by itself on the top of the mud—so up I rid, and being a bit jubus, I lifted it with the butt end of my whip when a feller sung out from under it, Hallo, stranger, who told you to knock my hat off? Why, says I what sort of a sample of a white man are you? What's

come of the rest of you? Oh, says he, I'm not far off—only
in the next county. I'm doing beautifully—got one of the
best horses under me that ever burrowed—claws like a
mole —no stop in him—but here's a waggon and horses
right under me in a mighty bad fix, I reckon, for I heard
the driver say a spell ago one of the team was getting a
leetel tired.[13]

In 1951, Vance Randolph reported finding the tale still in oral
tradition:

Tall stories about mud are still common in [Eureka Springs, Arkansas].
One of the old tales concerns the traveler who saw a man's hat in a pud-
dle, picked it up, and found a be-whiskered head underneath. Shocked
and surprised, he grabbed the man by the collar and tried to help him
out of the mud. "Let me alone, stranger," cried the hillman, "you're a-pul-
ling me right out of the saddle."

A variant of this yarn is about the city fellow who found a fine Stetson
in a quagmire near Rolla, Missouri. He got a long pole to drag the hat
within reach, but soon discovered that there was a man's head under it.
"Good God, you're in a bad fix!" he cried. The man in the mudhole shook
the water out of his eyes. "Yeah, I *shore* am," he admitted. "It's lucky I've
got a good horse under me, or I might have got kind of damp."[14]

Other variants have circulated, too. In 1943, Sergeant Bill Davidson's collection of *Tall Tales They Tell in the Services* recorded the same
deep mud story, except that the GIs had replaced the horse with a
jeep.[15]

Motifs travel across the centuries; stories and techniques drift back
and forth between folklore and a large body of literature; the idea of
a national humor grows around a peculiar mode of storytelling. Through
the motion and commotion we can see patterns, forming an aggregate
image of the American tall tale, though we can never completely disen-
tangle the oral from the written. There is a folk tall tale and there is
a literary tall tale, but they have closely entwined histories, methods,
aesthetics, and functions. If we cannot with certainty trace particular
folkloric influences on writers and on individual literary works, we can
look for generic methods and meanings. And if we cannot study
nineteenth-century folklore first-hand, we can study its modern de-
scendant. So looking backward from Don Lewis to Mark Twain or Davy

Crockett gives us not a clear distinction between folk and literary influences, and not the long view of historical progression in either folklore or literature, but a sharper view of individual tales, events, and works of art—a view of the humor, of the powerful communication of values, and of the cultural and psychological usefulness of the tall tale.

CHAPTER 2

Stretchers, Yarns, and Windies:
A Genre of the Folk

Now here's a true one. . . .
—Among others, Jim Griffith, National Folk Festival, 1977

The Problem of the Tall Tale

When Don Lewis answered a mother's innocent question about snakes with a tall tale, he placed her in an uncomfortable position. Very likely the camper's mother was puzzled by the strangeness of Don Lewis' yarn, surprised to hear such a tale coming from an apparently reliable person, and bothered by the moral atmosphere in which it was told—an atmosphere in which the line between fact and fiction is hazy and the manipulation of that boundary is a source of humor. At the very least she probably puzzled over how much, if any, of the information could be relied upon as fact. If she was puzzled and bothered by the tall tale, she was not the first.

In 1856 Jim Bridger—explorer, guide, trapper, and yarnspinner—described the Yellowstone area's geysers, hot springs, and other wonders to Colonel R.T. Van Horn, editor of the *Kansas City Journal*. Van Horn took notes and intended to publish the account until "a man who claimed to know Bridger, told him that he would be laughed out of town if he printed 'any of old Jim Bridger's lies.'" Van Horn suppressed the story, but then twenty-three years later publicly apologized to Bridger, for it turned out that on this occasion the tall-talking mountain man had, for once, told the truth.[1]

Today, folklore archivists also puzzle over the classification of strange narratives that may or may not be tall tales. The solution traditionally adopted by folklorists is to classify as tall tales only those humorous stories which contain clear impossibilities or gross exaggerations of natural phenomena, like the pumpkin vine that grew so fast the pumpkins had to be put on wheels to keep them from shattering, or the hunter who kills two animals with one shot by splitting the bullet on a sharp rock.[2] But because the yarnspinner's form imposes a kind of verisimilitude, because many strange things happen in this world, and finally because ideas of what is possible change with time and experience (as they did for Colonel Van Horn), outlandishness alone cannot reliably be used to identify the tall tale. We clearly need some other criteria for distinguishing and defining tall tales.

Folk narratives are generally divided into three categories by both folklorists and the folk cultures that create the tales: true narratives, fictional narratives, and truth narratives.[3] The true narratives—personal narratives, anecdotes about others, and accounts of community events—are told as true and heard as true. Though in style and structure the true narratives may be traditional, and though the events are filtered through the sensibilities of the narrator, the content is intended to be factual and listeners are expected to believe in them as factual. The fictional narratives—Märchen, fable, joke, trickster tale, ghost story, and so on—are told as fiction and heard as fiction. Truth narratives, sacred or secular myths, are not verifiable because of their remoteness from the present world, but are told and heard as cultural truths that account for the otherwise unaccountable, and are generally believed as facts by narrator and listeners.[4] Now there are two types of narrative which cannot be neatly placed into any of these categories. The legend is a fictional tale both told and heard as true. Often set in the very recent past, it deals with ordinary people who encounter the extraordinary or the mysterious; and though it cannot be verified it calls for strict belief. The tall tale, finally, is a fictional narrative, told as fiction. Its peculiarities are, first, that it masquerades as a true narrative, for it is told in the form of a personal narrative or an anecdote, and, second, that it is sometimes heard as true, not simply through the mistakes of children or fools but by the design of the narrator. Finally, listeners who hear the tall tale as fiction often act as though they believe it to be true.

We may begin, then, not with a definition that simply calls the tall tale a comic lie or an impossible exaggeration, but with the notion that the tall tale is a fictional story which is told in the form of personal narrative or anecdote, which challenges the listener's credulity with comic outlandishness, and which performs different social functions depending on whether it is heard as true or as fictional. The more fully we can elaborate this definition, the more confidently we will be able to identify tall tales, whether told by Baptist camp directors or tall-talking mountain men.

The Search for the Tall Tale

The tall tale is difficult to trace through history, but it has surely been around a very long time. The *Odyssey* must have its sources in oral yarn-spinning, and we catch very regular glimpses of the tall tale in literature from the first century A.D. onward. Its continuity, too, is remarkable. The story about words which freeze and cannot be heard until they are thawed was perhaps first recorded by Plutarch (c. A.D. 46–120):

Antiphanes said humorously that in a certain city words congealed with the cold the moment they were spoken, and later, as they thawed out, people heard in the summer what they had said to one another in the winter.[5]

It appears again in Castiglione's *Book of the Courtier* (1528), when a character reports a story, "affirmed as positive fact," about merchants shouting across the frozen Dnieper, unable to hear one another. Finally some local people, who have seen this happen before, build a fire out on the river's ice and thaw out the words.[6] Four hundred years later, one J.O. Lobb of Nebraska "noticed his brother's words freezing. [He] caught some of them in a sack, and carried them home and thawed them out by the fire.[7]

Between Plutarch and Lobb, the tall tale can be traced primarily in its more formal manifestations, such as medieval lying contests and a sixteenth-century liars' club whose proceedings were recorded by one of its members.[8] The most famous European yarnspinner was Baron Münchausen, who achieved an unwanted renown when R.E. Raspe, a scholar and discredited public functionary, published *Baron Münchausen's Narrative of his Marvellous Travels and Campaigns in Russia* (1786). Raspe based his original pamphlet on his acquaintance with both the real baron and the German literary traditions of extravagant fictions and Lugendichtungen (poems of lying).[9]*Münchausen*, repeatedly enlarged and revised by later editors, was so successful that by 1800 it had been translated into five languages[10] and by 1835 it had been through twenty-four American editions.[11]

Despite the success of *Münchausen*, the actual popularity of the tall tale in eighteenth- and nineteenth-century Europe is difficult to assess. Although serious collecting of folklore by folklorists began in the nineteenth century in Europe, the tall tale was largely ignored. The pioneering folklorists—Jacob Grimm, John Francis Campbell, Max Muller, Andrew Lang—conceived of folktales as relics of ancient Indo-Germanic mythology, and concentrated on explaining the mythic origins and symbols of tales. This orientation drew them more strongly to the Märchen than the tall tale, which, however traditional, *seems* to grow more directly out of contemporary life. In the twentieth century, the European tall tale has received more attention from folklorists, and has been recorded by researchers like Gustav Hennigsen, whose "The Art of Perpendicular Lying" presented a collection of Norwegian sailors' yarns.[12]

In the United States the tall tale has flourished in both folklore and folklore collecting. By 1966, when Ernest Baughman compiled his *Type and Motif-Index of the Folktales of England and North America*, more than half of the types and motifs collected by folklorists in America were humorous, and most of these (3,710 out of a total of 3,871) were tall tales. Among the 3,966 tales collected in England and Lowland Scotland, only twenty-nine were tall tales.[13] Of course tall tales have been more avidly sought in America than elsewhere, and the apparent concreteness of these figures may be seductively deceptive. Nonetheless, the numbers support what intuition believes: the Americans have established the tall tale as a national form and a potent inspiration to their culture.

One qualification must, however, be offered here. The tall tale is primarily a white male form. Though Black people do tell tall tales, as Zora Neale Hurston has shown in *Mules and Men* and *Their Eyes Were Watching God*, and though a rare female tale teller or two have

Liars' contests and folk festivals often bring together yarnspinners of disparate backgrounds before an audience of friendly strangers. Here Jim Griffith (*right*), a yarnspinning folklorist, shares the stage with his friend Van Holyoak (*left*), a poetry-writing, tale-telling cowboy, at the National Council for the Traditional Arts' National Folk Festival in Vienna, Virginia, 1978. Photo by Carolyn Brown.

been found, Blacks have found greater satisfaction in trickster and bad-man tales, and white women have more often participated in tall tale sessions as appreciative listeners or deliberate ignorers and scoffers. Whatever the reasons, the collections of folklorists, as well as the literary tall tales, deal almost exclusively with white male storytellers, for whom the tall tale has been the favorite form of humorous narrative.[14]

The records of early American tall tales are informal, often incidental. The earliest records are those of tourists and travelers who ran across yarning and tall-talking Americans along the way. Local traditions carried down through the years the reputations and tales of talented yarn-spinners. Some of these were eventually recorded in town annals, like this one from Washington, New Hampshire, written near the end of the nineteenth century:

Our town in those distant days, had its men of eccentric character, its story teller, one who was especially gifted in the power to entertain by the re-cital of scenes and adventures which it was not essential for the hearer to believe in order to enjoy. The elder Farnsworth, who had a family of six-teen children, was an inveterate taker of snuff, and could likewise tell a good story,

"such as of Salmon in his boots,
Full sixty pounds he drew,"

and once in an encounter with a bear, after fighting for two hours on a large stump of a tree, he—not the bear—came off conqueror and killed a bear and a cub.[15]

Folklore as an academic discipline pursued by trained fieldworkers matured in the United States only after the turn of the century. In the 1920s Archer Taylor published several significant works on folktales and the Finnish historic-geographic method of folktale study, and in 1928 Stith Thompson published his translated and enlarged edition of Antii Aarne's *The Types of the Folktale*.[16] In this atmosphere of growing professionalism, scholarly studies of the tall tale (as opposed to literary re-creations and adaptations) began to appear.

Some of these modern folklorists supplement our anecdotal records of the nineteenth-century tall tale, reaching backward in time by inter-viewing the younger contemporaries of great nineteenth-century yarn-spinners. William Hugh Jansen's 1949 study of Abraham "Oregon" Smith, an Illinois yarnspinner, documents the storytelling of a man who, dying in 1893 at the age of ninety-seven, had been a contemporary of Davy Crockett and Jim Bridger, as well as of George Washington Harris and Mark Twain. Because many of Jansen's informants had known "lying Abe" and remembered hearing him tell the tales, Jansen was able to gather not only the tales but also comments on Smith's style, the social situation, and the reaction of the audience. Some of the informants were themselves accomplished raconteurs with a gifted sensitivity to the techniques of successful storytelling.[17]

The tales of Gib Morgan, another nineteenth-century yarnspinner, were recorded by folklorist Mody Boatright. Morgan, an oil driller and Civil War veteran who died in 1909, spun yarns about his travels and drilling adventures, which were then repeated and probably augmented as they spread through oil fields from Pennsylvania and West Virginia to Texas and Oklahoma. Like "Oregon" Smith, his fame was long lasting, though by 1945 Boatright found that the stories were "hardly known except among a generation of oil workers becoming fewer each year."[18]

Mody Boatright also collected miscellaneous tall tales told by a great variety of frontier yarnspinners. In *Folk Laughter on the American Frontier* he observes that the frontiersman "lied in order to satirize his betters; he lied to cure others of the swell head; he lied in order to initiate the recruits to his way of life. He lied to amuse himself and his fellows. He was an artist, and like all true artists his chief reward was in the exercise of art, however surcharged it might be with social or other significance."[19]

Of course the frontier has no patent on tall tales. In Maine, a yarnspinner of a more restricted fame and a more domesticated life—Jones Tracy of Mount Desert Island (1856–1939)—used to lure dancers away from parties and down into the kitchen to hear his long, tall stories. His tales were collected a generation after his death by Richard Lunt, who detected a change in the tall tale in that community. When his informants described or told Jones Tracy's tales, the yarns were long, complex, and filled with realistic detail. Their own tales, created and told in a modern culture that places more pressure on their time, were shorter and inclined toward the joke form.[20]

Not long after Jones Tracy's death, Herbert Halpert published his study of "John Darling, a New York Munchausen" (1944), describing a man who made verbal artistry a vocation as well as an avocation. According to Halpert's informants, "he used to be quite a preacher they say John was. Just went from one schoolhouse to another. Said he was a great preacher—holler and take on," but he was also "the damndest liar in seven states."[21]

The tall tales of more contemporary yarnspinners have been recorded directly by folklorists, who are then able to observe first-hand not only the tales but also the interactions between narrator and audience. One of the most infamous sites for tall yarnspinning is the Ozark mountain region of Arkansas, where Vance Randolph found yarnspinners who took particular delight in victimizing tourists for the amusements of the locals. The tales about bad weather, poor crops, and small hogs in *We Always Lie to Strangers* are accompanied by descriptions of the hill people puzzling and astonishing the tourists:

> Some of the finest windies are never told directly to the tourist; it is better to allow him to overhear them, as if by accident. Frank Payne and W.D. Mathes, of Galena, Missouri, used to make a specialty of this technique. They would talk together in low tones, very seriously, with their backs toward the "furriner" to whom the story was really addressed. These men were artists, and people came from miles around to see them do their stuff.[22]

Tall tales told in the Okefenokee Swamp Rim, studied by Kay Cothran, are used not for the befuddlement of tourists but as a weapon in the skirmishes between the sexes and between the local social classes. Cothran found that among her informants the tall tale is not just an amusement but a statement about modern middle-class culture.[23]

For Ed Bell, a bait store owner on the Texas Gulf Coast, tall tales are an important asset to his business: the tales attract people to the store and then make them feel like fishing. According to Partick Mullen, who collected some of these tales in *I Heard the Old Fisherman Say*, Ed is known as far as fifty miles away and is called "one of the biggest liars on the Texas coast."[24]

The tale tellers in these and other standard folklore studies represent a far greater number of tall tale narrators who have spun their yarns in all times and places in America. So one need not search among oil drillers or mountain farmers to find tall tales. My own fieldwork in the late seventies turned up several yarnspinners in central and western Virginia: Don Lewis, summer camp director; Brandon Deane, a University of Virginia student who was also a native of Charlottesville; "Rob-

bie" Robbins, a student from North Carolina; Christopher Stubbs, another University student, but half-American and half-British and raised
in the Middle East; Luther Napier, my illiterate country neighbor who
was either an outright liar or a yarnspinner with a deadpan so convinc-
ing that I'm still confused; and various strangers about whom I know
nothing but that I once overheard them tell a tale.

Contemporary yarnspinners can also be found at toastmasters' clubs,
local liars' contests, and folk festivals such as the National Folk Festival
in Vienna, Virginia, where I interviewed two visiting Arizonans: Jim
Griffith, a yarnspinning folklorist, and Van Holyoak, a storytelling,
poetry-writing cowboy.

Though these yarns and yarnspinners were found in different times
and places by collectors with varying skills, methods and motives, together
they will allow us to form a composite portrait—a portrait of the
humorous, extravagant, credibly-incredible, entertaining, socially binding, and excluding American tall tale.

The Texts of Tall Tales

The telling of any folktale is a communicative event, a complex inter-
twining of text and context, form and function. To attempt to separate
the inseparable is sometimes enlightening if one approaches the task
with a sense of humor, proportion, and humility, expecting the division to be neither clean nor permanent but simply and temporarily
useful. Let us, for now, call "text" the plot, the action, and the words
of a tall tale. And let us call "context" the social situation, the interactions between teller and listeners, and the function (both personal and
social) of the tale-telling event. The narrator's manner and textural de-
vices must be considered along with both text and context.[25]

The text of a tall tale is, first of all, cast in the form of a true narrative
and filled out with supporting details from the narrator's everyday life.
If the yarnspinner himself is not the hero, he tells the story about his
best friend or, perhaps, his grandfather. In any case, he presents his
tale as a spontaneous reminiscence. Gib Morgan, the oil driller, so skillfully introduced his tales into the immediate situation that different
people claimed to recall different occasions as the time that Gib first
"made up" certain stories.[26]

The facade of factuality is most often supported by the deadpan style. One of William Jansen's informants, who remembered "Oregon" Smith from his boyhood, distinctly recalled Abe's solemn demeanor:

He never cracked a smile when he told his tales *and* he didn't want you to smile either. He was no fool. Why the world produces people who'll tell stories like that like they were the truth, I don't know. He was reprimanded often enough, goodness knows. . . . Us kids would listen to him by the hour. But it made him mad [was this not acting?] when we would laugh. He'd say, almost fierce, "What's so funny about that, son?" (Jansen's brackets).[27]

The deadpan is not, however, universal. Many a narrator will laugh at the end of a solemnly told tale to assure listeners that he intends to amuse, not deceive, or perhaps to assure them of his sanity. Although Don Lewis generally affects the solemn tone, when he spins yarns before children he often grins or winks to help them understand the tall tale form, to avoid excluding them from the joke.[28] In the Okefenokee Swamp Rim, Kay Cothran found even among adults a "grinning, mobile faced" style, though the words of the tale still insisted upon its factuality.

Beyond the requirement that he cast his fiction in the form of true narrative, the yarnspinner is not restricted by any single conventional structure. Because his story must appear to be a spontaneous reminiscence, and because it must be adapted to his own life, and finally because it often grows out of real experiences, the tall tale genre requires a form more flexible than the structures of many other folktale types.

Some whoppers cannot legitimately be called narratives at all because they contain no plot or narrative movement.[29] Barre Toelken reports such an encounter between an eastern tourist and two desert service station attendants. When the tourist asked, "Does it always get this hot around here?" the mechanic replied, "Well, when it *really* gets hot in these parts the farmers start feeding cracked ice to the chickens to keep 'em from laying hard-boiled eggs."[30] Descriptive, as opposed to narrative, whoppers are not always one-liners. Some ramble at length, moving from one impossibility to the next, expanding or explaining the basic absurdity introduced at the beginning. When Don Lewis felt the demonic inspiration to comfort an uneasy mother by telling her that the snakes at her son's camp are mostly eaten by mountain lions, her gullibility urged him on through a lengthy disquisition:

"Tell me," she said, "Do y'all have much trouble with snakes?" And I said, "No, ma'am," which was true, we don't . . . Now we've seen a lot, of course, but y'know, they're at a distance, and most of the time you see their tail end 'cause they're leaving. . . . So I said "No ma'am, . . . we really don't." I said, "The mountain lions eat 'em." And I get this weird look from her, you know, and I see this one guy, we had a, the same trip we had this forester who was with us, and he looked at me and all I could see was a little twinkle in his eye, just this tiny—he never cracked a *smile* . . . and there was something about that that just kinda triggered the whole thing in me, and we get off on this wild story about mountain lions and the fact that they don't have retractable claws. (Which is true. As I re-call it is anyway. It may not be, but it was true when I was telling it.) And the reason is, you see, that the claws grow, just like a beaver's teeth, or any rodent's teeth grow, and they have to gnaw. Well the claws on mountain lions grow and they have to dig. Well that makes it ideal, because they can dig down into the dens of snakes, which are their favorite food. And they can kill the snakes, and they're not bothered by the snake's poison at all, unless the snake gets them on the ear. So it's quite a battle, y'know, they've got to keep their ears [out of the way] and that's why they have small, rounded ears on mountain lions, not anything big a snake can grab onto. Well this story went on and on, and y'know it got bigger and bigger and the more it went the more I felt sorry for the lady because she was be-lieving me. And it was also, you know we have to run two or three tours on Monday, and we have a limited amount of time, and I was running out of time to tell them something else, but I just couldn't get stopped; it was just so much fun!

Though they have no narrative structure, these unplotted whoppers present a fiction in the guise of fact, use typical tall tale textural de-vices, and serve several of the functions of the tall tale. Perhaps they should be called by the more general term, tall lying, rather than by the more common, though less accurate term, tall tale. Following cus-tom, however, and wishing to emphasize that these whoppers are told as fiction and not lies, I will continue to use the term tall tale, remark-ing only that the whopper and the narrative are structurally different, but substantially the same.[31]

Structure in the narrative tall tales can be more successfully analyzed. Many of them are constructed of three to five elements: three plot stages, with optional prologue and coda. Often a tale begins with a claim that it is true or a statement expressing the narrator's distaste for liars. In many societies a conventional Märchen opening indicates to the listener that what follows is fiction and should not be believed;[32] the tall tale's traditional opening assertion of factuality seems to indicate that the tale *does* call for belief, though of course it is also a clue that what follows will be fiction. The tale itself generally begins with realistic detail designed to establish the credibility of the story. The second major stage describes a series of events increasing in absurdity or in their distance from ordinary life. Finally, the tale reaches its climax and, in some tales, a resolution. Many yarns end on their most impossible point—"the Injun killed me" or "so I went home and got a shovel to dig myself out." Sometimes the climax will be followed by another formulaic assertion of truth. When Ernest Hobbs tells the traditional tale about large mosquitoes and an iron kettle, he follows this pattern of increasing absurdity, impossible climax, and formulaic ending. "The mosquitoes down there," he begins, "I mean, those are really what bothers us, you know." Mr. Hobbs then describes a swarm of mosquitoes: "you can hear 'em comin' nigh onto twenty miles away . . . they sound like dive bombers." Emphasizing the exaggeration with understatement, he claims that "they aren't too big—about as big as maybe a buzzard would get, you know." Mr. Hobbs then explains how his grandfather, trying to escape the mosquitoes, hid under an iron kettle. When the insects drilled through the kettle, Grandfather bent their beaks over inside. Unfortunately, the mosquitoes then picked up the kettle and flew off with it. Having reached his climax, Mr. Hobbs quickly finishes off the tale with "It *is* a fact."[33]

The closing assertion of truth may also be less direct. One tale told both by and about Abraham "Oregon" Smith describes him carrying a bed sack full of shot out of a burning hardware store and sinking into the stone pavement at every step. Sometimes Abe would say, "They told a lie on me about that fire. They said I sank in the pavement up to my knees. That wasn't true. It was only up to my ankles. The tracks is there yet . . . the tracks is there yet."[34]

Often a tale that seems to end on its most impossible point will be capped by another speaker who provides a resolution either by undercutting the first speaker or by adding an even more absurd claim. Tales about huge vegetables, for example, may be followed by a tale about the manufacture of a huge iron pot. When the first speaker asks what such a pot could possibly be used for, the second liar replies "Why to cook your turnip, of course."[35]

In a variation of this basic structure, instead of building to a climax the tale may wind down to a humorous understatement. Don Lewis told one such tale in response to my remark that I had heard that the local bobcats could talk:

Some of our bobcats are more intelligent than others. Now some of 'em are really sneaky, and they're very good hunters and so on. Most of them make by with a living; you know, they kinda get by, but that's about it. But we do have some, now there was one guy was up here one time, and he didn't believe the story about the talking bobcats. He thought we were pulling his leg. But . . . he ran into one. Well, the thing was he really wasn't talking at the time, but what he ran into was he came up here and it was on a Sunday morning, and somebody'd left one of the Camp Craft manuals out, and he found that this bobcat was up here reading it. He was up here and had his, you know he was sittin' up here on the picnic table reading the thing, and the guy came back and told me about it, and he was just astounded. He said, "I *saw* this bobcat reading," you know. But it's typical of somebody from the city, because he just makes certain basic assumptions about things in the woods, you know, because he got out here, and he sees this bobcat reading, and right away he assumes it's an abnormally intelligent bobcat. But I got a description from him and I *know* the bobcat. He's not really that smart, 'cause I mean he can't even read without moving his lips . . . It's a terrible [thing to say?], you know, but he's not bad; I mean he *can* [read] . . . mostly comic books anyway. You really have to watch that. They do walk off with a lot of our comic books.

After the comment about the bobcat moving his lips, Don continues speaking, allowing the tale to fade back into the rhythms of ordinary conversation so that it will not sound like a joke with "moving his lips" as its punchline.

The structure and the balance of realism and fantasy in the tall tale depend largely, then, upon the artistry of the teller, his purposes, and the circumstances and inspiration of the moment. Because of this essential flexibility, the tall tale cannot be defined by structure. While the presence of a typical tall tale structure may help to identify it as a windy, an unusual construction will not exclude a story from the tall tale family. A clever narrator can adapt an appropriate motif to whatever structure best suits the occasion.

The motif from which a tall tale is spun may be either traditional or original. The story of a hunter who kills many animals with one shot has been collected in Nebraska and Missouri as well as in Europe.[36] Such stories move through space and time, each narrator changing the details to suit his circumstances, personality, and reputation, adapting it to his own life and telling it as if there were no traditional tale. Meanwhile, new tall tales continue to be invented. Some of these, no doubt, circulate in folk tradition and will be recorded in future indexes. Others are personal enough that they remain attached to the particular yarnspinners who created them.

Whether a tall tale be infinitely varied by innumerable narrators or spontaneously told once and then forgotten, it is often inspired by an actual but unusual event. When Jim Bridger discovered the Obsidian Cliff, a mass of volcanic glass, he worked it into a now famous hunting story which, unfortunately, was not recorded in his own words.

Coming one day in sight of a magnificent elk, he took careful aim at the unsuspecting animal and fired. To his great amazement, the elk not only was not wounded, but seemed not even to have heard the report of the rifle. Bridger drew considerably nearer and gave the elk the benefit of his most deliberate aim; but with the same result as before. A third and fourth effort met with a similar fate. Utterly exasperated, he seized his rifle by the barrel, resolved to use it as a club since it had failed as a firearm. He rushed madly toward the elk, but suddenly crashed into an immovable vertical wall which proved to be a mountain of perfectly transparent glass, on the farther side of which, still in peaceful security, the elk was quietly grazing. Stranger, still, the mountain was not only of pure glass, but was a perfect telescopic lens, and whereas, the elk seemed but a few hundred yards off, it was in reality twenty-five miles away![37]

Don Lewis also bases most of his tales on actual events. One night as he and a counselor called Crunch were walking through the woods, near the Peaks of Otter, they heard an extremely large animal rushing toward them. When Don shone a light in its direction, the large animal veered and they saw only a chipmunk scampering away. When Don later told the story of their fright in the woods, he explained that he had been terrified but Crunch had pushed him out of the way of the 200-pound Wild Bull Chipmunk. The story was later elaborated so that the chipmunks were blamed for stomping the potholes into the camp roads and were given credit both for graveling the roads by butting their heads against rocks and for clearing the hiking trails by knocking down oak trees ("I mean, how many acorns, y'know, would one of these things eat?").

Inspired by real events and circumstances that are somehow odd, incongruous, or extreme, the narrator then exaggerates the unexpected to make it humorous and even more outrageous. The exaggeration in tall tales—the extravagance of the fiction—ranges over a broad continuum from the mildly improbable, through the physically impossible, to the mind-jarringly illogical. This continuum should not be confused with a scale of truthfulness, for an improbable tale may be entirely fabricated, while an impossible or illogical tale may contain a good deal of emotional or even factual truth. Furthermore, any tall tale is told as a fiction. The differences lie only in their *apparent* distance from the everyday world.

Illogical exaggeration contains what Gilbert Ryle, in a very different context, called the category mistake. Although the sentences are syntactically correct, the category mistake creates an absurdity by allocating an object or a concept to a logical type or category to which it does not belong.[38] In the illogical tall tale, the humor arises from the intellectual disorientation experienced by the listener when he recognizes or attempts to reconcile the category mistake. In the old story claiming it was so cold that a man's words froze as he spoke, the category mistake consists of treating words as objects which can freeze. An illogical tale about deep holes and strong wind treats a hole as something which can exist without a substrate and be acted upon in the same way that a tree or post can be acted upon:

Holes? My grandfather had a well 200 feet deep, but the gravel around it was sandy and a windstorm blew it away and left the hole up 200 feet in the air. He had his sons-in-law saw it up and they used it for fence-post holes.[39]

One of Jim Bridger's illogical tales began with a true premise—the existence of petrified wood—then elaborated the idea far beyond the limits of reason. The story tells of the petrified canyon where "Jim's mules broke their teeth trying to eat petrified grass, where the sun had no warmth because sunlight was petrified, where petrified birds sang petrified songs, where Jim had once escaped the Blackfeet by riding straight off through the air because even the law of gravity was petrified.[40]

Occasionally a narrator will surprise his listeners by disguising an illogical tale as a milder form of exaggeration. A traditional story about a champion jumper, for example, may at first seem to be simple exaggeration of the man's ability. Van Holyoak told this one about his grandfather, who tried to jump the Grand Canyon once when it got in his way:

He backs way off and got 'im a good run . . . he run right up to the edge of it and made 'im a merry hell of a jump, 'n he lacked about twenty feet of gettin' to the far side of it, and seen he wasn't gonna make it so he turned around and went back.[41]

If Van's grandfather were swimming, this might be a numbskull joke. If the tale described in hyperbolic terms how the jumper got back, it would be an impossible tall tale. But since we are left to picture him sauntering back shame-faced, the humor derives mainly from the category mistake which compels us to contemplate the absurdity of sauntering back through mid-air.

The tall tales most commonly collected by folklorists have been those in the impossible range of the exaggeration scale. Often they exaggerate the strength, intelligence, or viciousness of animals: a clever hunting dog digs worms when the hunter goes fishing; mosquitoes, when driven off, retreat to the hillside and throw rocks. Vance Randolph repeats a typical extravagance reported by Fred Blair in a pamphlet on Arkansas: when the farmer came out to chase the bears from his cornfield, "the bears fled, walking on their hind legs, with armloads of green corn, and big pumpkins balanced on their heads."[42] Rough weather also inspires large exaggerations. Roger Welsch describes a Nebraska wind vane made from a twelve-foot logging chain hung from a post. His informant explained that the wind direction was determined by watching which way the chain was blowing, and added, "we could tell the wind was really blowing when links began to snap off the end of that chain."[43] Even more outlandish is the tale about weather so hot that the corn popped in the fields, and the cows, thinking it was snow, froze to death (Baughman, Motif X1633.1).

Toward the realistic end of the continuum of exaggeration lie tales which may seem impossible or only mildly improbable, depending upon the experiences of the categorizer, and may even, to some, seem not to be tall tales at all. Robbie Robbins, when he was a student at the University of Virginia, used to tell such comic but not wholly incredible tales about some well-known bears who inhabit the Great Smoky Mountains National Park. Kamikaze Bear once charged down the hillside and crashed through a cabin wall to get at the food locked inside by wary campers. Equally bold was Suicide Bear, who dove out from a tree limb to pull down a bag of food the campers had hung twenty-five feet above the ground. At the Peaks of Otter, a camp counselor named Brandon Deane often created comic whoppers that belong to the realm of the possible-but-outrageously-false. A little nervous about his upcoming marriage, and a little embarassed about a trip to the city to get his marriage license, he told Ronnie (a fifteen-year-old junior counselor with a reputation for gullibility) that he was going home to get his "learner's permit." "Do they really give you a learner's permit?" Ronnie was at this point somewhat suspicious, but Brandon was ready for the challenge: "Sure. Then you can try it out for awhile, and if things work out, after a month you get married. You can even get a learner's permit with one of the names left blank so you can try out several different people and see who you like best." What is appealing about Brandon's stretcher, and what places it akin to the tall tale, is not a radical departure from fact, but the humorous presentation of fiction in the form of fact, the comic exposure of his ambivalent attitude toward marriage, and the use of what I will call the tall tale conceit.

Like the metaphysical conceit of the seventeenth-century poets, the tall tale conceit compares its subject to something strikingly different; but the tall tale conceit creates the comparison comically, absurdly. The tall tale does not simply exaggerate, describing mosquitoes three or eight or ten feet long, but concretely and comically compares, telling how they sound like dive bombers and can be heard "nigh onto twenty miles away." Or it anthropomorphizes animals in comically absurd detail, comparing them to the most clever and mischievous of humans, explaining perhaps how the adult grasshoppers ate the turnips "as far down into the ground as they could reach, and then let the younguns down on ropes to devour the taproots."[44] Or it more directly transforms one object into another, most often in the illogical tales, telling of the time it was so cold that the fire froze and the hero broke it up and used it for pepper. But the tall tale conceit need not create an impossibility. Brandon Dean's "learner's permit" whopper modestly but whimsically deflates the legal technicalities of marriage and turns romance to humor with a curious comparison.

The "learner's permit," the story of Kamikaze Bear, and other tales which stay even closer to the possible or actual experiences of life, would not be called tall tales by many folklorists, who have traditionally reserved the term for stories which are grossly exaggerated and distinctly false. Folk narrators, on the other hand, generally recognize the improbable tale's close kinship with the more easily recognized and labeled impossible tale. Dewey, Ernest, and Virgil Ray, for example, tell traditional tall tales, numbskull stories, trickster stories, and what collector Brunhilde Biebuyck-Goetz calls "folklorized" personal experiences — all of them presented as if they were actual personal experiences and all of them called "lies" by the three brothers.[45] The numbskull and trickster motifs and the personal experience stories are cast into the form of tall tales, use the textural devices and techniques of verisimilitude of the tall tale, are told as fictions, are told in the same context as the brothers' traditional tall tales, are called the same name, and seem to serve the same social functions. Are they not, then, tall tales which have simply borrowed their subject matter (motifs) from other genres?[46] Generic criticism has never greatly concerned itself with the sources of an artist's material. The definition of genre depends upon the form of the work and the rhetorical relationship between the artist and his audience.[47] If, therefore, a narrative based upon personal experience exhibits the textural, structural, and functional characteristics of a tall tale, if it is told as a humorous fiction rather than a factual account, it is a tall tale, no matter how true it is or how close it stays to experiences possible in the real world. Its real meanings are indirect and symbolic; its real pleasure is in the artistry of the telling.

In any of these varieties of the tall tale — improbable, impossible, or illogical — the plot and the characters, as well as the exaggeration, are intended to be comic. Morton Gurewitch, in *Comedy: The Irrational Vision*, outlines four modes of comedy:

Traditional satire excoriates folly, finding it ridiculous but also corrigible. Humor seeks, not to expunge folly, but to condone and even to bless it, for humor views folly as endearing, humanizing, indispensable. Farce also accepts folly as indispensable, but only because folly promises delightful annihilations of restraint. Finally, irony sees folly as an emblem of eternal irrationality, to be coolly anatomized and toyed with.[48]

The comedy in tall tales is probably least often ironic. Most tall yarn-spinners find too much joy in their yarning to create the coolness or bitterness of irony. More often the tall tale is warmly humorous, celebrating the humanness of people who find, create, or must cope with absurd situations. Certainly there may be satire in tall tales that ridicule the ignorance of outsiders or try to correct the mistakes of newcomers. Don Lewis' mountain lion and snake yarn gently satirizes the naïveté and the unreasonable fears of the worried mother, and then slides into farce as his imagination elaborates the notion of mountain lions eating snakes. Often in farcical tall tales it is not action but imagination which runs wild in "delightful annihilations of restraint." Mosquitoes as large as buzzards and as loud as dive bombers, or bears that carry armloads of corn and balance pumpkins on their heads clearly belong to the realm of farce.

When the unrestrained energy of farce leaps the bounds of ordinary categories or when it yokes together laughter and repulsion, it becomes grotesque. Vividly grotesque tall tales seldom make it into print, even in the collections of dedicated folklorists. Sandra Stahl managed to collect one, though, from Larry Scheiber of Huntington, Indiana. The story tells of a fishing trip Larry took with Tiny Wires, who claimed that the best bait for catfish was chicken blood.

This stuff had all congealed, and it looked sorta like liver. I didn't know chicken blood would do that, but, but it hangs right on your ol' hook, ya know? You get a great big glob of that crap and ya cast out, and it hits the water ["kafush!"—plus motion with hand]—Skawat!—and it just sinks 'cause ya put weight on it. And ya just set there and set there and pretty soon—tug, tug, tug—and ya reel in a catfish.

Larry soon became too disgusted to participate and "set up on the bank and drank beer." Finally he said, "let's go back and get some broads or something and drink beer and tell lies . . . So we went back to his house, and naturally I got to carry the bucket again. And I stuck it under the [house] trailer. And this was, oh, I don't know, about June. Long about July [pause]—[laughter] . . . the neighbors started complaining. . . ." When Larry finally discovered the bucket under the trailer heaving with maggots [here his listeners groan], they dragged it out and determined to toss the bucket into the river as they drove slowly over the bridge. At the climax of the tale, Larry throws the bucket, it hits the bridge railing, and blood and maggots splatter all over the car and all over Larry, who is hanging out the window.

He rolled the window up on me, powered the window (whrr—). There I am hangin out by my waist, ya know. "Let me in Wires, ya son of a bitch," I says, "I'm getting crusted!" [Laughter] You know, the wind was drying me off and those things were cakin on me. [Laughter] Then he drives up to the car wash. Still won't roll down the goddam window. I says [in a strained voice], "What are ya gonna do?! And he puts in the quarter and [makes noise of water jetting from hose]. He uses the high-pressure water bit. Maggots flying all over the place. The whole bottom of the car was full of maggots. 'Cept they wouldn't come off the car. That was the *goodest* part. He had to go home and get 'em off with a putty knife. [Laughter] I layed there in the yard just laughin.[49]

Through the tale, Larry's audience responds with alternating groans and laughter. Although the exaggeration in this tale is only of the improbable variety, the comedy is unrestrained by notions of politeness, good taste, or rational behavior; it revels in man's ridiculousness.

Underlying all types of tall tale comedy is the comic contrast between the pretense of absolute, literal factuality and the outrageousness of the material. As the narrator dallies at the border between the credible and the incredible, his success depends less upon the distance between fact and tale than upon his use of tall tale artistry: the deadpan pose, the variations of rhythm and timing, the sharp realistic detail, the absurd tall tale conceit, the comic understatement, the vivid naming (Wild Bull Chipmunk, Kamikaze Bear), the skillful manipulation of the listener's values and beliefs. The best yarnspinners are also comic actors. When Don Lewis was a boy, he spent hours in his room whispering, practicing jokes and tales in front of the mirror. Today he fills his stories with action—hand movements, facial expressions, and vocal sound effects. Often he also, in order to enhance the "good ol' boy" effect, exaggerates his southern accent and loosens up his grammar. Each narration is a performance carefully crafted and continually adapted as he watches his audience's reaction.

The interplay of these textural elements with the structure of a plot can be seen in one of Don's stories about the Norwegian rats that take over the camp staff house during the winter months. The tale also displays some of Don's pleasure in the imaginative freedom of farce and demonstrates how actual experiences can be turned into tall tales. The story was inspired by two separate incidents. On one occasion Don did shoot a rat at close range with an overly powerful gun. And one dark night there *was* a rat involved in the collapse of a cot, and as he fell Don was slapped on the face with the loose end of a coiled climbing rope. The story turned out something like this:

Well we had some good size rats, there for a while, at the staff house that we had to shoot out. We had one that . . . well, when I first got there in the staff house, the first year I came up here, there was alota rats, and we shot, oh I guess, four or five out. Originally I shot 'em with a .22, but I began to realize it didn't make much difference on the older ones. So I got to where I was using a .30–.30 on 'em, because otherwise, they'd just, you know, you plug 'em and they just go down the hole and that was it. So you'd blow 'em off with a .30–.30. There were a couple bigger ones, though. You know, it was really kinda dangerous, because if you didn't hit 'em just right, get a good heart shot on 'em, if you hit 'em, you know they'd crawl off and then you'd have to go after 'em. And you know people talk about goin' after a wounded deer, but, man they don't know anything about danger till you go after a wounded rat. That's all there is to it. So you've really got to watch out for some of them. Now we had one big one that just scared the daylights out of me one night. I was sleepin' on one of these spring things, you know one of these bed springs, like the army had, you know. And you know how they fold underneath, the legs'll fold up underneath? Durn near killed me. Scared the daylights out of me. I was setting there asleep and I heard this (scraping sound) across the floor and I knew he was a good size rat, but I just didn't realize how good size he was. Well, as he went by I looked up, and I thought it was a small bear goin' by, you know, 'cause he was right good sized. But . . . you know you just can't get excited at things like that 'cause it just doesn't pay. And besides which, I had, you know all my food was there up in that room, cause I'd just come in for the weekend. So I, I got ticked off, beaned 'im with m'flashlight, told him to get out of the room. So he gets up to leave the room—see he was all scared too; he didn't like human beings. Rats are pretty secretive—even when they're large they're secretive, you know. And, course I guess everybody's aware of that. But at any rate, he, uh, got banged up side the head with that flashlight, and I yelled at 'im. I didn't realize how big he was, or I wouldn't never of hit 'im with my flashlight. Well he tried to get out the door. He'd come in this other way, and he tried to get out the door . . . and got stuck. He made it through the front end, but if you ever looked at a rat, their hips are real big in the back, you know. And he kinda got wedged in a bit. Well, he had trouble gettin in or out, really. He coulda backed out some, but I was back there, and he was get- tin' panicky, and course he started thrashin' and his tail came, and came right on in and just smack right on the bottom section of those legs on the cot. Just flipped the thing, you know, so the legs went underneath, the cot came down, I rolled out, it was pitch black and—absolutely scared me to death. It was like wrestlin' with an alligator; you had to stay out of the way of the tail . . . as long as you did that, it was ok. He finally got out all right, but he ripped out the left side of the door jamb. It cost me 25 bucks to replace the durn thing.

Though not Don's most imaginative production or his most skillful presentation, this story illustrates many common tall tale techniques. It begins with a plausible, somewhat rambling introduction. The first hint of exaggeration comes with his explanation of the kind of gun used to shoot the rats. To some of Don's audience—youngsters, female suburbanites—the use of a .30–.30 on a rat might be questionable but not entirely incredible. The introductory material ends with a solemnly stated affirmation of the danger of encountering a wounded rat. As Don begins the action of his tale, he describes the cot, preparing the listener for the climax and giving some suggestion of what it will be. Obviously, to stop and describe the cot a the point of its collapse would destroy the flow of words at the tale's climax. Don's imitation of the swishing, scraping sound of the rat walking across the floor is typical of the way he embellishes his tales with sound effects. These sound ef- fects, voice modulations, and rhythmic changes are as important to the tale as they are impossible to convey in a transcript.

When he describes a rat the size of a small bear as "right good size," Don uses the classic tall tale mixture of gross exaggeration and under- statement. The succeeding comments, though apparently extraneous, reassert the attitude of seriousness: "But . . . you know you just can't get excited at things like that 'cause it just doesn't pay. And besides which, I had, you know all my food was there up in that room." So Don hit the rat with his flashlight. Next comes another seemingly serious comment about the secretiveness of rats. Don loves to lace his tales with the lore of the amateur naturalist. The details (most but not all of them true) increase his credibility and provide humorous contrast to the blatantly exaggerated parts of the tales. Now, as imagination escapes the fetters of the probable, the size of the rat grows. The annihilation of restraint, in both action and imagination, produces the farcical image of Don clubbing a bear-sized rat with his flashlight.

The next section of the tale contains the fairly straightforward narration of the climax of the story. Don simulates the excitement of the moment by increasing his tempo up to the quick, regular rhythm of the series "the legs went underneath, the cot came down, I rolled out, it was pitch black and—[break] absolutely scared me to death." The pace then gradually slows and the last two sentences are stated in a voice of calm resentment. The final remark about fixing the door jamb realistically validates the fiction. Although this is meant to be a comic tale, it has no punch line; it gradually eases out of and then back into the ordinary affairs of everyday life where it costs twenty-five dollars to repair a broken door jamb. And although there is a farcical element in the action, most of the humor resides in the contrast between the solemn tone and the clear falsity of the material—the tall tale pose of a fictional story told as true.

There is more, however, than comedy in the Norwegian rat story. In this and other tales about the uncertainties of man's interactions with nature, Don simultaneously admits and makes light of his fears, and often the fears of his listeners. For both narrator and audience, tall tales have important psychological and social uses which become more clear when we examine the tales in context.

Contexts and Functions of Tall Tales

"For a work of art to be effective," says Roger Abrahams, "it must not only communicate with an audience, but it must also excite its participation. Both communication and participation are a matter of drawing upon the deep cultural matrix within the individuals in the audience. The idea that lies behind performance is a remarkably simple one: to set up rhythms and expectancies which will permit—indeed, insists upon—a synchronized audience reation. This places the burden upon the performer to establish those expectancies, but in this he is aided by his traditions, both in formal and in symbolic dimensions."[50] A tall tale narrator sets up these expectations in his audience by choosing texts, structures, and language typical of the tall tale. He also draws upon and replays traditions of situation and context, and he uses the tall tale to perform traditional social and psychological functions.

The tall tale is, first, a play form, a game designed to entertain and amuse. Our ninteenth-century commentators often depict it being told in barrooms, on steamboats and stagecoaches, beside campfires, and from the loafers' bench in front of the general store. In the Okefeno-kee Swamp Rim, Kay Cothran found that tall tales are told primarily by rural men who, working by the sun and the seasons rather than by the middle-class townsman's clock, have leisure that seems appropriate to tale telling.[51] In Alberta, Herbert Halpert found wilderness guide Scotty Wright telling tall yarns to his clients around campfires, and Alex McTavish and his cronies spinning tales at branding time, "particularly when some greenhorn or tenderfoot — an eastern visitor, was present."[52] The rural loafer, the western guide, and the frontier farmer fit the stereotype of the tall tale narrator as a member of a subculture on the geographical or social fringes of the larger culture, but in fact the tall tale enlivens informal gatherings across many regions and social classes. Brandon Deane, middle-class resident of a small southern city, told extended tall tales and practiced elaborate hoaxes in that epitome of leisure environments, the summer camp. In town or among his university friends, in a busier environment, Brandon still laced his leisure moments with exaggerated quips and short, spontaneous tall tales. Though he adapted the length and kind of tale to his immediate social situation, in both groups Brandon filled the role of joker and storyteller.

Such tale tellers may slip a single tale into an otherwise ordinary conversation, or they may stretch the entertainment out into a long storytelling session. Many yarnspinning sessions are dominated by a soloist, someone, like Abraham "Oregon" Smith, recognized as a virtuoso raconteur and sought out to entertain the group unaided and uninterrupted. In other sessions group members may share equally in the entertainment. During cooperative storytelling sessions, speakers reinforce or verify one another's tales, while in competitive sessions they challenge one another's skill in a mock-solemn exchange of outrageous fabrications. Richard Lunt reports that Jones Tracy, provoked by someone's boast (or tale) about very large, sweet apples coming from a small tree, told of burying an anvil under an apple tree: the tree produced two armored cruisers and a battleship.[53] In Nebraska, Roger Welsch found that tall tales were often "told in an exchange sequence, each liar trying to outdo the last, but never laughing at even one's own tale. During such exchanges," Welsch explains, "there may be a silence between the stories, as if the audience were pondering the wonder of the event just described — but the pauses are more likely to recall even more amazing tales."[54]

Often such a yarnspinning group will collaborate in practicing their art before strangers. Alex McTavish described how, at branding time, a story might be told in the greenhorn's presence, perhaps started by one speaker and then enlarged by others. "They would tell it as a matter of course — just part of the daily conversation. . . . Naturally, if he had any brains at all, he would savvy that they were having fun at his expense."[55]

McTavish's description points up the tall tale's frequent dependence upon some sort of tension between insider and outsider, old-timer and greenhorn, although the old-timer may be either old or young, urban or rural. All folk groups, from oilmen to academicians, have their own folklore and may, if they have a talented yarnspinner among them, have their own tall tales. In considering the tall tale as the property of a folk group we move beyond the notion of the tale as a form of entertainment. Like many forms of art, the tall tale is, in the Burkian phrase, equipment for living.[56] It serves two important functions: it promotes and reinforces group identity, and it provides a means of controlling threatening situations by reshaping them into fantasy.

A folk group is, according to Barre Toelken, a "high context group," a group sharing "extensive informal communal contacts."[57] A folk group is also a group of people sharing a self-image — primarily an image of their values which differ, or appear to differ, from the values of other groups.[58] Whether the group members have a common ethnic heritage, occupation, or hobby, their shared knowledge and values distinguish them from nonmembers and imbue their tall tales with meanings peculiar to the group. Here is where the yarnspinner makes use of Abrahams' "deep cultural matrix" to elicit the participation of his audience. Although the city-bred reader may be able, on some level, to understand and enjoy the Ozark tall tales reported in Vance Randolph's *We Always Lie to Strangers*, his appreciation is limited by his distance from the tale's total context. Explanations by the author and the general modern technological spread of information in our larger culture can inform him of what a razorback hog is and looks like, but a tale about a razorback can never have the same meaning for the reader that it had for the folk group in which it arose — a group which makes part of its living by raising hogs. Likewise the humor in hunting yarns often depends upon a knowledge of weapons, dogs, and the habits of the game, and might be meaningless or puzzling to an outsider. In the nation's oilfields, the original wide geographic spread of the Gib Morgan stories may be attributed to the commonality of oilmen's experience, and the subsequent disappearance of the tales is probably due less to the mere passage of time than to changes in the techniques, experiences, and concerns of oil drillers.

As the narrator uses the group's peculiarities of experience, knowledge and values to draw his listeners into the tale, he also reinforces group identity—sometimes by proudly flaunting the group's self-image. Tall tales about poor soil or rough weather inflate the hardiness of those who can cope with such troubles, and thereby imply the inferiority of those who need not. The tale about a well hole being cut up and used for post holes, in addition to creating humor through the conjunction of incompatible concepts, celebrates the perseverance and ingenuity of the frontier farmer.

In some situations the mere act of tale telling accomplishes this distinguishing of folk groups. Kay Cothran found a deliberate and pointed exercise of the tall tale's power to separate groups in the Okefenokee Swamp Rim:

Talking trash as a custom comes from a time when men did not work by the time clock but by cycles of nature. Talking trash today is an act of identification with that older way of life, and, whether one does it as a matter of course or as something of rebellion, talking trash is a sneer at middle-class subservience to continuous gray work and a denial of that class's identification of the materially unproductive with the counter productive.[59]

The Swamp Rim women and the upwardly mobile townspeople felt the need to repudiate the tall tale traditon as unproductive, old-fashioned, and uncivilized, although they might vicariously enjoy the tales.

In other communities, too, there are people who understand the fictionality of a tale but remain only partly amused and somewhat uncomfortable. In New York, most of the people who told Herbert Halpert about John Darling recognized that Darling's deadpan delivery of his tales was part of his art, but at least one informant was offended by Darling's insistence that the stories were factual.[60] William Jansen found that some of the people who most appreciated Abe Smith's art felt obliged to assure the visiting folklorist (obviously an outsider who might misunderstand) that Abe was honest and religious and never expected anyone to believe his tales. Others in the community considered Abe's lies to be purposeless, harmful, and immoral.[61] Clearly such community members do not fully share the values of the even smaller folk group to which the tale really belongs.

Sometimes a group's self-image suggests tall tales which never come to full fruition. At the University of Virginia a small group of outdoor enthusiasts for a couple of years (1977–78) used their specialized knowledge of rock climbing, mountaineering, and other sports to develop a corpus of "Robbie Stories"—exaggerated, humorous tales about the unfortunate exploits of one of the group members. Because of their esoteric content and vocabulary, the tales delineated an elite group: only the initiated knew and understood the stories. Interestingly, the stories did not portray Robbie as an ideal but instead implied the ideal through comic contrast. Although in reality he was quite competent, the tales depicted Robbie as inexperienced and clumsy and lacking in common sense—all potentially disastrous traits in a mountaineer. To those who knew the hero, understood the sports he engaged in, and could see where he made his mistakes, the tales were quite funny. Yet the tallest Robbie story of all was that there were so many Robbie stories. They were really quite few. Although the people involved wanted to have Robbie stories, to fill their need for this kind of group identifier and unifier and perhaps to exorcise their own mistakes and anxieties, they had no master yarnspinner among them to create a large body of satisfying tales. Still, the exaggeration of the number of stories was in itself a kind of tall tale that had significant meaning to the group. So powerful is the tall tale that even where artistry is lacking, the idea of a tall tale may still bind and identify a folk group.

As the tall tale binds and identifies a folk group, it also offers outsiders a way of joining. While one important function of folklore of almost any type is the initiation of group novices, the tall tale initiates new members only if they play the game properly. The tale assumes a quick wit and a familiarity with the genre and the subject matter, and operates as a test of that wit and knowledge. The outsider who never comprehends the humorous intent of the tale, or who perceives it and is offended, remains an outsider. The tall stories told at the Baptist summer camp, for example, challenge the boys to recognize the difference between fact and fantasy in the woods, and then provide them with a symbol of their common initiation. The boys who understand about talking bobcats or who know about the zitflitter, a battery acid-eating bird, form an alliance which distinguishes them from those who do not.

While it reinforces group identity and initiates new members, the tall tale may aggressively exclude outsiders. In the fantasy world of the tall tale, conflicts between groups are projected through humor rather than open hostility, and tensions may be either exercised or dissipated by making a game of the ignorance of outsiders. When the audience actually includes an outsider, such as the tourists who run into Vance Randolph's Ozark farmers, the narrator attempts to conquer the outsider by manipulating his feelings and beliefs, by wholly or partly fooling him.

Sometimes, rather than serving to exclude outsiders, the tall tale can establish a temporary intimacy between strangers because it allows the perceptive listener—though not a candidate for initiation—to see and understand a part of the world of the narrator. Don Lewis discovered this long before he became a camp director. In the late sixties, several years before backpacking exploded into a popular sport, Don and a friend were hiking on the Appalachian Trail, and at a point where the trail intersects the Skyline Drive they stopped to speak to a tourist who knew nothing about hiking or camping and who thought of the two young men as real woodsmen. The story that Don spun for this tourist told of a hill so steep the hikers were forced to put their packs on in front, to keep from being pulled off the hill. Finally, upon reaching the top, they realized that "the durn thing was overhung." Don's comments on this tale explain how such a story may create a momentary friendship between people of different backgrounds and experience:

He begins to realize that you're pullin' his leg, and he knows it. And yet he knows you're sharing something, too. He also knows you probably did hit a bad hill. And so he begins to get fascinated by it, because in a sense you've opened up your world to him. And granted you're pulling his leg; granted you're telling this tall tale, and he knows it, but in a sense it's almost like you're expected to do that, too.

If the novice or outsider can enjoy the role of gullible victim, and if the narrator can generously accept the outsider's good will, the tall tale need not be an expression of hostility or an attempt to manipulate; it may be simply a celebration and a sharing of unusual experiences.

Yet even when the tall tale does not mock the values and ignorance of outsiders, it generally mocks or defies something. With an attitude of exuberant irreverence toward the trials of life, the narrator becomes superior to circumstance by casting it in a comic form. In other cultures and other contexts, the Märchen, the geste, and the etiological tale create fictional worlds which reduce the apparent disorder of the universe. André Jolles explained that the Märchen takes place in a world that is specifically described as different from and better than ours. The tale is ethical in its orientation, depicting a world in which justice is done.[62] Unlike the Märchen, the tall tale occurs in an amoral world, where survival and humor are more important than ethics. The world of the tall tale is worse than our world, though not in a malignant way; and control and order are imposed not through some higher scheme of justice or some supernatural agent, but by the artist's control of his fiction and by his attitude toward his material. Even when he seems to create a greater chaos, the tall tale narrator subdues disorder with irreverent laughter.

An attitude of irreverence toward the threats of nature governs many of Don Lewis' tales which are based on absurd things that happen in the woods. In the woods, Don believes, man has less control over his world than he has in a more civilized environment. The stories, then, are "an attempt to make some kind of sense or maybe a joke or do away with a little bit of the threat of a disorganized universe." In the Wild Bull Chipmunk story, Don expresses his fear not simply by reliving it but by exercising artistic control over it. He recreates the moment, shaping it to his own fancy, exaggerating it to comic proportions, laughing at it, and thereby conquering it.

The best of these tall tale narrators hold special positions in their folk groups. They are "characters": self-created fools or heroes who triumph over nature, fear, stress, or outsiders through wit and artistic creation, and who border on social deviance because of their attitude toward the larger culture or their nonchalant approach to the distinction between fiction and fact. In southern Indiana and eastern Illinois, Abe Smith attracted assemblies of listeners simply through his reputation. Country boys come to town would follow Abe around waiting for him to release a tale, and adults at political rallies gathered about him with the same hope.[63] Such men are performers, entertainers who will spin yarns for the joy of it even without the promptings of natural disaster or intergroup tensions. They tell tales simply because they have some need for exhibition, or some desire for comic self-definition, or

simply because, through some quirk of genius, preposterous ideas occur to them. As Don Lewis explained to me when he told me about
the mother who worried about snakes, the tall tale narrator often cannot say why he has lied, except that an unusual situation or a gullible
person gave him the opportunity and then, once he had begun, he
"just couldn't get stopped; it was just so much fun!"

The tall tale has neither a simple definition nor a single function:
in its finest manifestations it is too complex a work of art and artistry.
But it can be described more fully and accurately and be recognized
more confidently than it often has been. How can a Kansas City newspaper editor, a young camper's mother, or even a folklorist distinguish
fact from fantasy, personal narrative from tall tale? He or she cannot,
always. But if there is a certain sense of outlandishness; if there is a
movement from the realm of the realistic and probable to the improbable, a dalliance at that hazy border between the credible and the
incredible; if there are tall tale conceits and exaggeration through
understatement; if there is a sense that the tale delineates an "in"
group and challenges the listener to prove himself clever or dull, in or
out of that group through his response to the tale; if the narrator seems
to relish the role of comedian, social deviant, or mocker of hardship
and danger, and seems to be manipulating the bizarre happenings of
real life to make them his comic servants; if these are the traits of the
story and the atmosphere of the storytelling event, then the narrative
had best be considered a tall tale.

CHAPTER 3

Flush Times:
Varieties of Written Tales

A new vein of literature, as original as it is inexhaustible in its
source, has been opened in this country within a very few years,
with the most marked success.
                            —William T. Porter, 1843

Whether in a barroom or at a boys' summer camp, the yarnspinner who
knows how to tell a good lie creates not just a tale, not just a comic exaggeration, but also a character, be he wit, hero, fool or rogue; and he
also creates a distinct, peculiar relationship with his auditors, be they
strangers, acquaintances, enemies, or lifelong friends. So too, the writer
who would successfully adapt the tall tale to print must make his tale-
teller not just a type or a dialect-speaking voice, but a realizable character. And he must evoke (perhaps create, since he is a writer and not
a folk narrator) an implicit set of values and a common experience
which can be stretched and exaggerated, creating that tall world which
exists at the border between the credible and the incredible, pushing
sometimes slightly and sometimes very far beyond that implied normal
experience. In the best tall tale literature, the author does even more:
he or she creates this tall tale atmosphere and establishes the tall tale
relationship not simply among the characters but between the author
and the readers. In the nineteenth century, particularly during the
flush times of 1831 to 1860, a long and numerous procession of writers
flooded America's periodicals, almanacs, and books with written tall

tales which created compelling tall narrators and established this tall tale relationship in varying, complex, comic ways.

Certainly there were signs and beginnings and even full-fledged tall tales in print before 1831. Americans were telling tall tales all along in their homes, taverns, stages, and camps, and the tallness occasionally slipped into print. In 1728 William Byrd's *History of the Dividing Line betwixt Virginia and North Carolina* described and exaggerated what the Virginia gentleman saw as the extraordinary indolence of the North Carolinians.[1] Benjamin Franklin, whose humor concentrated on homely aphorisms, crackerbarrel philosophy, and sophisticated imitations of the *Spectator*, nonetheless understood and occasionally captured in print his countrymen's delight in tall humor. In one newspaper spoof he claimed that the American sheep's "very tails are so laden with Wool, that each has a Car or Waggon on four little Wheels to support and keep it from trailing on the Ground." He then described the preparations for a cod and whale fishery in the Great Lakes, and claimed that "the grand leap of the Whale . . . up the Fall of Niagara is esteemed by all who have seen it, as one of the finest Spectacles in Nature."[2] Though this kind of humor appears infrequently in Franklin's writing, such well-turned tales must have been created by a man practiced in the art of oral yarnspinning.

By the early nineteenth century, the tall talk of real-life southwesterners began to be recorded in popular literature. In a travel book published in 1810, Christian Schultz reported an exchange of boasts between two riverboatmen;[3] in 1821 Alphonso Wetmore depicted the tall-talking boatman Mike Fink in *The Peddlar;* and in 1822 the song "the Hunters of Kentucky" caught the national imagination as an expression of exuberant patriotism. Clearly business was picking up.

By 1830 the idea of distinct, stereotypical regional characters was firmly established, available to be thrown in the face of European cultural snobbery, as in Paulding's *The Lion of the West* (1831); contrasted with other regional characters, as in many of the *Spirit of the Times* sketches; or set against a genteel norm, as in Longstreet's sketches of Georgia scenes (originally published 1827-35). During the next several decades, newspapers like the *New Orleans Picayune*, the *St. Louis Reveille*, and the (New York) *Spirit of the Times*, along with almanacs and popular anthologies, overflowed with tall literature from every section of the country. Most of the writers were professional men — lawyers, soldiers, editors — intent on recording the language, habits, and humor of peculiar local types and characters. Their most difficult task was to create, from the regional stereotypes, individual, compelling characters and to capture in print the maneuvering, manipulating, challenging, and entertaining relationship between tale-teller and audience. Some of them stuck very close to actual tales heard, reporting rather than inventing. Others created characters, tales, and tale-telling situations from a combination of memories and personal fancy. Among them, they developed a corpus of forms and techniques for creating the literary tall tale.

The Sketch

Protesting that he presented nothing more than "fanciful *combinations* of *real* incidents and characters," Augustus Baldwin Longstreet— lawyer, judge, newspaper editor, and later college president—in 1835 published a collection of sketches and essays that inaugurated the flush times of the American literary tall tale. Originally published separately in Georgia newspapers, the collected *Georgia Scenes* were immediately popular in both the South and the North; Longstreet came to be classified among the distinguished southern writers; and later sketch writers excused their backwoods subject matter by citing the example of "the great Longstreet."[4] These fanciful combinations of real incidents are not exclusively tall tales. The book's sections are too disparate, and it owes too much to literary tradition, especially to the Addisonian essay, for any such simple classification. But in the combination of Baldwin and Hall, in the contrast of city and backwoods, in the conjoining of elevated prose and rustic dialect, Longstreet creates a Georgia out of which tallness can, and occasionally does, grow.

Longstreet establishes the potential for a tall tale relationship first by indicating the credentials of the author and his two narrators. The title page ascribes the book simply to "A Native Georgian." Among Georgians, this sobriquet establishes the author as an insider, free to criticize, joke, and yarn about his native region. To outsiders, the "native Georgian" is one who ought to know (and claims, in the Preface, to tell) the truth about a state which, to the antebellum North, seemed mysterious and uncivilized. The individual sketches are signed, as they were in the original newspaper publication, with either of two pseudonyms: Baldwin or Hall. Lyman Hall and Abraham Baldwin take their names from two early Georgia patriots[5] and thus possess the right to describe, explain, criticize, and exaggerate. Their snatches of autobiography reveal that both grew up with the maturing civilization on the frontier and abandoned the rural life in search of education, culture, and fame. Both thus exercise a dual vision: an acquired taste for civilization, enlivened by a sentimental attachment to and a real appreciation of rustic simplicity and vigor. Baldwin and Hall between them create a world of values upon which the tall tale can operate.

Baldwin is conservative, commonsensical, Addisonian.[6] His gently moralistic essays probe the foibles of polite society by sketching type characters: a mother silly with her child but rude to her servant, a young lady who is a "Charming Creature" but a miserably incompetent wife, travelers who become enamoured of cacaphonous French and Italian music, young fops who duel over an imagined insult to a vain young lady. Though his tone is not strident, he pokes and prods thoughtless social conventions, imitativeness, and self-centered posing:

Here the seconds separated, and soon after the principals met; and Crouch shot Noozle, in due form and according to the latest fashion, through the knees. I went to see him after he had received his wound; and, poor fellow, he suffered dreadful tortures. So much, said I, for a young lady's lingering from a ball an hour too long, in order to make herself conspicuous. ("The Ball")[7]

Baldwin's disapproval of modern music, dancing, fashions, and manners is offset by his admiration for amiable and competent housewives; plainspoken, hardworking farmers; and modest but forthright country girls. Observing the preparations for a country dance, he poses the rhetorical question, "Which is entitled to the most credit; the young lady who rises with the dawn, and puts herself and whole house in order for a ball four hours before it begins, or the one who requires a fortnight to get herself dressed for it?" (13). As the dance guests arrive, Baldwin demonstrates a clear distaste for "the refinements of the present day in female dress": the country girls "carried no more cloth upon their arms or straw upon their heads than was necessary to cover them. They used no artificial means of spreading their frock tails to an interesting extent from their ankles. They had no boards laced to their breasts, nor any corsets laced to their sides; consequently, they looked, for all the world, like human beings, and could be distinctly recognised

THE BIG BEAR OF ARKANSAS,

AND OTHER TALES.

EDITED BY WM. T. PORTER.

PHILADELPHIA: CAREY & HART.

1845.

William T. Porter encouraged the writers of tall tales and backwoods sketches by publishing their work in his weekly paper the *Spirit of the Times* and then by reprinting the best of the sketches in a series of anthologies. The illustrated title page for *"The Big Bear of Arkansas" and Other Sketches* shows Jim Dogget standing by while his dogs struggle with the mysterious "she bar" in the lake. The illustrations for this volume were done by Felix Octavius Carr Darley. Courtesy of the Clifton Waller Barrett Library of the University of Virginia Library.

as such at the distance of two hundred paces" (14). In Baldwin's view, modern civilization, as represented by Europe, the northern cities, and their southern imitators, does not necessarily confer superiority of morality or sense. Longstreet, we must remember, originally published many of these sketches in his paper, the *State Rights Sentinel*, and was a fervent advocate first of nullification and later of secession. His Baldwin sketches call for a culture based not on imitation of the North but on an indigenous southern dignity and simplicity. His contrast of excessive cultivation and rustic simplicity provides a two-layered vision of reality and normalcy against which Longstreet's tall tale Georgia can press.

Lyman Hall's vision is more complex, for he speaks in several voices. In "A Native Georgian," "The Wax Works," and "The Debating Society," he gaily describes the masculine recreations (mostly practical jokes) of his own class. His appreciation of "The Horse Swap" as a recreation for the rural lower class is similarly undiluted; but in other portrayals of backwoods pastimes—"Georgia Theatrics," "The Fight," and "The Gander Pulling"—he alternates vivid description with overly sentimental, moralistic reactions. This last is Longstreet's tall tale voice.

Longstreet's contrast between imported civilization and the more indigenous rustic society is based on the cliché, widely believed among his northern contemporaries, that the South was culturally backward and morally depraved. Letters and diaries of antebellum northerners explicitly reveal their preconceptions, their fear of southern violence and their belief in southern impetuosity. Upon arriving in New Orleans in 1841, for example, a young New Englander confided to his diary that, for the purpose of "money getting," he was "going regardless of consequences, into an unhealthy climate amongst lawless and vicious men."[8] Fifty years after Longstreet, a more famous southerner living in the North recalled the brutality of the stereotypical backwoods poor white of that period. He spoke through the voice of Huck Finn:

There couldn't anything wake them up all over, and make them happy all over, like a dog-fight—unless it might be putting turpentine on a stray dog and setting fire to him, or tying a tin pan to his tail and see him run himself to death.[9]

Longstreet, who studied at Yale and amused his friends there with anecdotes about Georgia, was well aware of his region's reputation.[10] His gander-pulling, eye-gouging, nose-biting Georgians elaborate the stereotype, filling it out with realistic detail. Having already baited the reader with claims of historical accuracy, the author then lulls him with a cultural cliché, and thus sets him up for a sell.

"Georgia Theatrics," which was written toward the middle of the series but placed first in the book, is something of a microcosm of Hall's work as a whole. It begins with the kind of precise detail more typical of the tall tale than the humorous essay, followed immediately by a statement of the narrator's moral preconceptions:

If my memory fail me not, the 10th of June, 1809 found me, at about 11 o'clock in the forenoon, ascending a long and gentle slope in what was called "The Dark Corner" of Lincoln. I believe it took its name from the moral darkness which reigned over that portion of the country at the time of which I am speaking. If in this point of view it was but a shade darker than the rest of the country, it was inconceivably dark. (p. 9)

The narrator's graceful prose aligns him with a world of order, optimism, and conventional feelings:

. . . its natural condition was anything but dark. It smiled in all the charms of spring; and spring borrowed a new charm from its undulating grounds, its luxuriant woodlands, its sportive streams, its vocal birds, and its blushing flowers. (p. 9)

Borrowing his imagery and diction from eighteenth-century poetry, the narrator characterizes himself as a man who sees the world through literary conventions that are soon to prove inadequate. The voices emerging from a nearby grove, in contrast, speak with the poetry of folk speech — sharp rhythmic bursts, alliteration, curses, and startling imagery:

"Oh, wake snakes, and walk your chalks! Brimstone and —fire! Don't hold me, Nick Stoval! The fight's made up, and let's go at it. —my soul if I don't jump down his throat, and gallop every chitterling out of him before you can say 'quit!'" (p. 9)

Hurrying toward the fight, our gentleman apparently arrives too late to prevent the victor from gouging out his opponent's eye. As he approaches, the "accomplices in the hellish deed" seem all to have fled. He sees only the victor retreating from the spot. Even in his horror and anger, his speech is conventional and stilted: "Come back, you brute! and assist me in relieving your fellow mortal, whom you have ruined for ever!" (p.11). This fight, however, turns out to have been only a game, a play with all the parts acted by a youth of eighteen, who was "just seein' how I could 'a' *fout.*" Though the youth's moral vision undoubtedly is dark, the narrator has been taken in, deceived by his own preconceptions about the southern backwoods way of life. Although some eye gouging probably did occur in the Georgia of 1809,[11] Longstreet's purpose is not to document it or to say how common he believed it to be. Instead, he warns us against passing judgments based on ignorance and narrow preconceptions. And he has introduced us into a world at the limits of our knowledge, where fact and fantasy are difficult to distinguish, and where ordinary reactions and judgments may be inapplicable.

The gander pulling was a nineteenth-century pastime well documented by contemporary writers, and Longstreet's sketch on the subject casts no doubt upon its nature or the fact of its existence. He does, however, contrast this rowdy and to many sensibilities brutal recreation with an overly sentimental regard for the sport's innocent victim:

The devoted gander was now produced; and Mr. Prator, having first tied his feet together with a strong cord, proceeded to the *neck-greasing.* Abhorrent as it may be to all who respect the tenderer relations of life, Mrs. Prator had actually prepared a gourd of *goose* grease for this very purpose. For myself, when I saw Ned dip his hands into the grease, and commence stroking down the feathers from breast to head, my thoughts took a melancholy turn. They dwelt in sadness upon the many conjugal felicities which had probably been shared between the *greasess* and the *greasee.* I could see him as he stood by her side, through many a chilly day and cheerless night. . . . Ye friends of the sacred tie! judge what were my feelings when, in the midst of these reflections, the voice of James Prator thundered on mine ear, "Darn his old dodging soul; brother Ned! grease his neck till a fly can't light on it!"   (pp. 113-14)

The abrupt switch to coarse dialogue brings the reader back to the idea of sport, with a jolt and perhaps a laugh. The narrator's true jocularity has already leaked out in his reference to "the greasess and the greasee" and it is now fully developed in his comic characterization of the competitors' horses.

Gridiron was a grave horse; but a suspicious eye which he cast to the right and left, wherever he moved, showed that "he was wide awake," and that "nobody better not go fooling with him" as his owner sometimes used to say. . . . Off they went, Miss Sally delighted; for she now thought the whole parade would end in nothing more nor less than her favourite amusement, a race. But Gridiron's visage pronounced this the most non-sensical business that ever a horse of sense was engaged in since the world began. . . . Gridiron, who had witnessed Miss Sally's treatment with aston-ishment and indignation, resolved not to pass between the posts until the whole matter should be explained to his satisfaction. He therefore stopped short, and, by very intelligible looks, demanded of the whippers whether, if he passed between them, he was to be treated as Miss Spitfire had been? . . . In the midst of the conference, Gridiron's eye lit upon the os-cillating gander . . . . After a short examination, he heaved a sigh, and looked behind him to see if the way was clear. It was plain that his mind was now made up; but, to satisfy the world that he would do nothing rashly, he took another view, and then wheeled and went for Harrisburg as if he had set in for a year's running. Nobody whooped at Gridiron, for all saw that his running was purely the result of philosophic deduc-tion.   (pp. 115-17)

When the gander's head has come off and the prize has been awarded, the winner and losers are reconciled by joking, drinking, and fighting, "after which all parted good friends." If the sketch has a moral, it is not that gander pulling is barbaric, for by the end the agony of the gander is long forgotten. If it has a meaning within the structure of the book, it is that an outsider's ordinary tastes and sentiments may not be compe-tent to judge the frontier life, and that the rewards of contact with the frontier come not from piously condemning but from accepting and appreciating the frontier and frontier tales on their own terms.

A sketch narrator who expresses and even seems to believe in conflict-ing values does not necessarily write tall tales, of course. In his discus-sion of Washington Irving's Geoffrey Crayon sketches, William Hedges explains that in most American sketches (as in much of American liter-ature) the narrator's response to people and places is of greater interest than the people and places are in themselves. Ultimately, the sketch reveals as much about the narrator as about his subject. In the case of Geoffrey Crayon, it reveals "a personality which does not fully compre-hend itself" and its own conflicts, a personality caught between the two extremes of European cultivation, dignity, and respectability and, on the other hand, American individualism, freedom, even irresponsibility.[12] The narrator of "The Gander Pulling" likewise feels the tug of conflicting value systems but has loaded his language in favor of the rough and ready frontier. He deliberately establishes the conflict in order to tease the reader, to make the reader himself feel that conflict, and to encourage him to choose, for the moment of the tale at least, tall humor over civilized notions of social responsibility.

One of Longstreet's most popular pieces, "The Fight," increases the frontier violence and so increases the potential for conflict between the narrator's stated values and his enjoyment of rough tales. "The Fight" depicts in great detail the kind of courthouse battle that was only imagined in "Georgia Theatrics." Having read the earlier sketch, do we now rush in, morally indignant like the narrator of "Georgia Theatrics," and condemn the characters? Do we treat this as documentary evidence that such fights commonly occurred with the full approval of families, friends, and peace officers? Do we swallow whole the narrator's claims of indignation? More likely we approach the sketch with skepticism and a sense of humor.

To establish his law-and-order pose, and perhaps to mollify any somber Georgians who might otherwise take offense, Longstreet opens and closes with assurances that his sketch is set "in the younger days of the Republic" and that "such scenes of barbarism and cruelty . . . are now of rare occurence." This temporal and moral distancing superficially free him of responsibility for an incident he delights in describing.

The narrator, Hall, clearly admires Billy Stallings and Bob Durham as physical specimens:

Billy ruled the upper battalion, and Bob the lower. The former measured six feet and an inch in his stockings, and, without a single pound of cumbrous flesh about him, weighed a hundred and eighty. The latter was an inch shorter than his rival, and ten pounds lighter; but he was much the most active of the two. In running and jumping he had but few equals in the county; and in wrestling, not one. In other respects they were nearly equal. Both were admirable specimens of human nature in its finest form. (p. 53)

Despite their positions as leaders of rival "battalions," Billy and Bob "were always very friendly; indeed, at their first interview, they seemed to conceive a wonderful attachment to each other." Hall deliberately demonstrates their lack of moral viciousness by contrasting them with Ransy Sniffle, a comic figure, degenerate both physically and morally:

Now there happened to reside in the county just alluded to a little fellow by the name of Ransy Sniffle; a sprout of Richmond, who, in his earlier days, had fed copiously upon red clay and blackberries. This diet had given to Ransy a complexion that a corpse would have disdained to own, and an abdominal rotundity that was quite unprepossessing. Long spells of the fever and ague, too, in Ransy's youth, had conspired with clay and blackberries to throw him quite out of the order of nature. His shoulders were fleshless and elevated; his head large and flat; his neck slim and translucent; and his arms, hands, fingers, and feet were lengthened out of all proportion to the rest of his frame. . . . His height was just five feet nothing; and his average weight in blackberry season, ninety-five. I have been thus particular in describing him, for the purpose of showing what a great matter a little fire sometimes kindleth. There was nothing on the earth which delighted Ransy so much as a fight. He never seemed fairly alive except when he was witnessing, fomenting, or talking about a fight. . . . Ransy had been kept for more than a year in the most torturing suspense as to the comparative manhood of Billy Stallings and Bob Durham He had resorted to all his usual expedients to bring them in collision, and had entirely failed. (pp. 54-55)

When a fight between Bob and Billy finally occurs, inspired by a quarrel between their wives and enflamed by Ransy Sniffle, they are surrounded by a cheering, tall-talking crowd. "Hurra, my little hornet!" they cry. "Oh, my little flying wild-cat, hold him if you can! and, when you get him fast, hold lightning next." As Bill and Bob tear at one another, biting off ears, flesh, and fingers, the crowd responds with joy and more tall talk:

"Look yonder!" cried the west; "didn't I tell you so! He hit the ground so hard it jarred his nose off. Now ain't he a pretty man as he stands? He shall have my sister Sal just for his pretty looks. I want to get in the breed of them sort o' men, to drive ugly out of my kinfolks." (p. 62)

Finally, with Bob atop him grinding dirt into his eyes, Bill cries "ENOUGH!" Meeting again two months after the fight, Bob and Billy shake hands and declare the dispute settled fairly:

"Bobby, you've *licked* me in a fair fight; but you wouldn't have done it if I hadn't been in the wrong. I oughn't to have treated your wife as I did; and I felt so through the whole fight; and it sort 'o cowed me."

"Well, Billy," said Bob, "let's be friends. Once in the fight, when you had my finger in your mouth, and was pealing me in the face and breast, I was going to halloo; but I thought of Betsy, and knew the house would be too hot for me if I got whipped when fighting for her after always whipping when I fought for myself."   (p. 64)

Though the fight between Bob and Billy is neither more nor less rational, the violence neither more nor less defensible, than the pistol duel in "The Ball," Longstreet shows that here, at least, a primitive kind of justice has been done.

The extraordinary strength and agility of the heroes, the tall talk, and the savoring of his region's supposed flaws, all indicate the inspiration of the oral tall tale—the triumph, indeed of tall tale over historical sketch. The closing sanctimonious judgment is by this point in *Georgia Scenes* formulaic:

Thanks to the Christian religion, to schools, colleges, and benevolent associations, such scenes of barbarism and cruelty as that which I have been just describing are now of rare occurrence, though they may still be occasionally met with in some of the new counties. Wherever they prevail, they are a disgrace to that community. The peace-officers who countenance them deserve a place in the Penitentiary.   (p. 64)

Though it partly reveals a genuine conflict in the mind of the sketch writer, this facade of moral outrage corresponds to the oral narrator's poker face: it is a disguise which, when penetrated by the clever, the open-minded, or the initiated, reveals humor. The notion that the dull, the narrow-minded, and the naïve might mistake these sketches for undiluted history and humorless moralizing adds another layer of humor—at least for Longstreet's Georgians, the real insiders to this joke. "The Fight" is, of course, a fiction, and in it Longstreet has created a self-consistent fictional world in which Billy and Bob are not villains or bullies but heroes whose strength, dignity, and good nature justify their violence, and a world in which Ransy Sniffle and the hypocritical Squire Loggins, safely fictional, can be safely laughed at.

Hall's clearest revelation of himself as a yarnspinner occurs at the very end of the last sketch in the book, "The Shooting Match." Traveling on horseback through a rural county, Hall falls in with a young man

named Billy Curlew. Eyeing Hall's good horse and fine clothes, Billy
attempts a traditional country man's ploy to assert his superiority over
snoopy, upperclass strangers. We know it today primarily as the "Arkansas Traveler." Hall, a former country man himself, turns the game back
on Billy.

"Good morning, sir!" said I, reining up my horse as I came up beside
him.

"How goes it stranger?" said he, with a tone of independence and self-
confidence that awakened my curiousity to know a little of his character.

"Going driving?" inquired I.

"Not exactly," replied, he, surveying my horse with a quzzical smile; "I
haven't been a driving *by myself* for a year or two; and my nose has got so
bad lately, I can't carry a cold trail *without hounds to help me.*"

Alone, and without hounds as he was, the question was rather a silly
one; but it answered the purpose for which it was put, which was only to
draw him into conversation, and I proceeded to make as decent a retreat as
I could.

"I didn't know," said I, "but that you were going to meet the hunts-
men, or going to your stand."

"Ah, sure enough," rejoined he, "that *mout* be a bee, as the old woman
said when she killed a wasp. It seems to me I ought to know you."

"Well, if you *ought*, why don't you?"

"What *mout* your name be?"

"It might be anything," said I, with borrowed wit, for I knew my man,
and knew what kind of conversation would please him most.

"Well, what *is* it, then?"

"It *is* Hall," said I; "but you know it might as well have been anything
else."

"Pretty, digging!" said he. "I find you're not the fool I took you to be;
so here's to a better acquaintance with you."   (pp. 197–98)

Billy is in fact on his way to a shooting match. And Hall, it turns
out, is the very man Billy's "daddy used to tell [him] about," who as
a boy won prizes in shooting matches against grown men. According
to Billy, Hall "was born a shooting, and killed squirrels before he was
weaned." Hall protests that his entire reputation was based upon two
chance shots, one of which won a handkerchief for Billy's mother. He
agrees, nonetheless, to accompany Billy to the match, only to find that
Billy insists he take a shot. Though at first "thunder-struck" by the idea
of shooting in the match, Hall finally resolves "to throw [him]self upon

a third chance shot," insisting always to the reader upon his inability and embarrassment. After all the other shots have been made, Lyman Hall takes his turn:

Policy dictated that I should fire with a falling rifle, and I adopted this mode; determining to fire as soon as the sights came on a line with the diamond, *bead* or no *bead*. Accordingly, I commenced lowering old Soap-stick; but in spite of all my muscular powers, she uniformly accelerated velocity. Before I could arrest her downward flight, she had not only passed the target, but was making rapid encroachments on my own toes. . . . I now, of course, determined to reverse the mode of firing, and put forth all my physical energies to raise Soap-stick to the mark. The effort silenced Billy, and gave tongue to all his companions. I had just strength enough to master Soap-stick's obstinate proclivity, and consequently, my nerves began to exhibit palpable signs of distress with her first imperceptible movement upward. A trembling commenced in my arms; increased, and extended rapidly to my body and lower extremities; so that, by the time that I had brought Soap-stick up to the mark, I was shaking form head to foot, exactly like a man under the continued action of a strong galvanic battery. . . . As soon as I found that Soap-stick was high enough (for I made no farther use of the sights than to ascertain this fact), I pulled trigger, and off she went.

After this display of weakness and ineptitude, the other men (and probably the reader) are astonished to discover that Hall's shot is second best—he has driven the cross at the center of the bull's eye. Hall jokes about the technique of shooting "with the double wabble," and expresses disappointment that his shot was only second best, but finally claims again that the shot was nothing more than good luck.

At this point, many readers may still be inclined to believe in their seemingly reliable narrator, especially since he makes himself out to be so humble and good-natured. We are amused, even, at Billy's simple-minded insistence on Hall's skill. But the closing paragraphs undercut our confidence, and suggest a new understanding of the story by revealing a new meaning in the narrator's name. The name Lyman Hall is taken from an early Georgian who signed the Declaration of Independence, and Georgia readers would initially have accepted the historical allusion and sought no further meaning. We find at the end, however, that this Ly-man may be a man who lies.

"Tell your mother," said I, "that I send her a quarter of beef, which I won, as I did the handkerchief, by nothing in the world but mere good luck."

"Hold your jaw, Lyman!" said Billy; "I an't a gwine to tell the old woman any such lies; for she's a *rael* reg'lar built Meth'dist"

The sketch then ends with an apparently unrelated remark. As Hall turns to leave, one of the men asks what office he is campaigning for. Though Hall assures him that he is not candidate, the man insists that all the "boys" will support him.

"Yes," said Billy, "dang old Roper if we don't go our death for you, no matter who offers. If ever you come out for anything, Lyman, jist let the boys of Upper Hogthief know it, and they'll go for you to the hilt, against creation, tit or no tit, that's the *tatur.*"

I thanked them kindly, but repeated my assurance The reader will not suppose that the district took its name from the character of the inhabitants. In almost every county in the state there is some spot or district which bears a contemptuous appellation, usually derived from local rivalships, or from a single accidental circumstance.

Upper Hogthief may have earned its name or reputation through a single accidental circumstance. But is Hall named Lyman by accident, and did he earn his reputation as a marksman with three chance shots? This final emphasis on lies, names, reputations, and accidents casts doubt back upon the entire sketch, emphasizing the question of the narrator's reliability without ever settling it. The oral tall tale seldom settles such matters, either: the listener must not expect to know at exactly what point and in what manner literal fact has given way to fiction.

Hall is, in the end, a yarnspinner who elaborates for the sake of a good story, who insists upon historical fidelity and then chooses a tall subject, who flaunts his region's flaws and treats them as strengths, who toys with the distinctions between cultural stereotypes and individual reality, and who genially challenges outsiders to distinguish among all of these.

Joining the tall tale and the Addisonian essay into one book, Longstreet depicted a Georgia of contrasts—a growing, changing state not to be easily classified or simplistically understood. He shows a region in flux, flowing and maturing from wildness to civilization, where there are still wild stretches awash with reckless fun and violence as well as

overly "civilized" inlets encrusted with pretensions and imported cor-
ruptions. Between them he implies, and partly depicts, a moderate
course, an American (though perhaps only Southern) golden mean of
homespun virtues, healthy recreations, and practical jokes that stop
short of violence. But he makes clear that his ideal of ethical and aesthetic moderation embraces the humor of straight-faced comic exaggeration, for he is a yarnspinner himself whose fictions pose as facts to
catch the unwary and delight the knowing.

The Anecdote

Longstreet creates his shifting, bifurcated vision—a known world verg-
ing into the comically unknowable, a realiable historian masking an unreliable yarnspinner—by manipulating cultural clichés, by contrasting
Baldwin and Hall, and by contrasting Hall's two or three voices. *Georgia Scenes* was accompanied by and followed by innumerable other literary tall tales whose authors found, of course, other ways to create tall
worlds and tall tale relationships.

The shortest and simplest of these were the tall anecdotes about
famous characters (real or fictional) that appeared in newspapers and almanacs; and the most numerous and popular anecdotes about a single
character appeared in the Crockett almanacs. Today the Crockett tales
seem repetitive in structure, uneven in artistry, and primitive in the evo-
cation of narrative context. Yet they were widely reprinted, and presumably read, during twenty years, from 1835 through 1856.[13] Their
popularity may be partly credited to the colloquial rhythms of the
prose and the occasionally striking imagery. In one tale Crockett tells
how he saved the world from an icy demise one morning when it was so
cold that

the airth had actually friz fast in her axis, and could'nt turn around; the
sun had got jammed between two cakes o' ice under the wheels, an' thar
he had bin shinin' and workin' to get loose, till he friz fast in his cold
sweat.[14]

The frigidity of the morning and the seriousness of the problem con-
fronting the hero are made clear not through simple exaggeration, but
through comic understatement: the sun personifed as a reliable but im-

perfect workman and the astronomical relations and distances reduced to a morning's walk over the hill. In another tale, Crockett describes a sound by evoking a striking, comic picture, a tall tale conceit which describes a grizzly bear whose "grinders made a noise jest as if all the devils in hell war sharpening cross-cut saws by steam power" (Dorson, p. 114). When Crockett finally closes with the bear he describes the fight in language that draws attention not to the pain of battle but to its own preposterous self. Having first shot the bear, Crockett must still drown him. Parodying folk names for rivers, he explains

I waited for him rite on the edge of Little Great Small Deep Shallow Big Muddy. He pitched inter me like the piston of a steam engine, and we both rolled into the drink together.

Tall tale visual metaphor is now followed by tall tale attribution of human emotions to animals:

Onluckily for him I didn't lose holt of Killdevil, and when he raised his head and tried to get over his astonishment, I clapt the barrel right across his neck to shove his visnomy under water.

In the everyday world we might say a bear was surprised, startled, or frightened, but probably not astonished. Then follows another preposterous image and the conclusion of the action:

I'll be shot with a packsaddle without benefit of clergy if the ridiculous fool didn't help me himself; for he clapped both hands on the eends of the barrel and pulled away as if it war a pleasure to him. I had nuthing to do but hold on the stock and float alongside of him till he war drowned.

Finally, Crockett again emphasizes that this is not something seen but something told, and alludes again to the comic humanness of the tall tale bear:

Don't you come for to say that I'm telling the least of a lie, for every fool knows a grizzly bear will live an hour with a ball through his heart, if so be he's only mad enuff.   (Dorson, p. 115)

In a more fantastic tale, Crockett sets out for Texas astride a fabulous bear that can outrun a thunderbolt. He arrives in a cloud of smoke and immediately sets into Santa Anna and "his whiskered shootin' flock." The Mexicans try to resist,

but it war no more use than a big goose hissing at thunder, for I out with
my bone scythe, an' if I didn't make Mexican heads fly about as thick as
horsechestnuts in a hurrycane, then melt me into iron for steambilers.

Here, again, is the tall tale conceit: striking, earthy imagery which exaggerates by yoking unlike things together in amusing ways.

Too often, however, the almanac stories exaggerate without the comic
imaginative language of the tall tale. In the nineteenth century the simple
act of printing or reading sub-standard language was somehow
humorous—a kind of oxymoron in itself. And so many a story in these
comic almanacs climaxes with some decidedly un-tall exaggeration:

So we wrassled an jerked and bit for a long time, till I got a chance at one
of his eyes with my thum nail. Then when I begun to put on the rail
Kentucky twist, he knew it was all day with him, and he fell on his knees
and begged for mercy.   (Dorson, p. 88)

Nor is the humor in these tales created by some carefully developed
narrative context. Even the best of the almanac tales leave the narrator's
identity sketchy and the narrative context uncertain. Who this Crockett
is and how he comes to be writing an almanac are neither explained
nor suggested in the tales. To the extent that they operated as tall tales,
rather than jokes, the almanac stories depended on a character and a
context that existed outside the tales. Davy Crockett was, after all, a
real person—or began as one anyway.

First elected to Congress in 1827, Crockett quickly became a cultural
and political symbol. To the Whigs he represented the ignorant riffraff
brought to power on Jackson's coattails; to the Democrats he embodied
the vigorous, unpretentious power of the Old Southwest. In James
Kirke Paulding's play *The Lion of the West*, first performed in 1831, the
Crockett character represents American character in a classic tall tale
victimization of European cultural snobbery. He plays the fool that the
lady tourist expects to find, and the success of his deception proves his
superiority. At the same time, the backwoodsman's boasts, tall tales,
and outlandish manners mask an essential nobleness.

Crockett cultivated the tall image, bowing to the audience from his
box (so they say) at a performance of Paulding's play,[15] and collabor-
ating on the *Sketches and Eccentricities of Col. David Crockett*, which
was freely embellished with hunting yarns and comic anecdotes. The
results were ambiguous; for although Crockett's fame grew, his political

strength was uncertain. His association with Paulding's Nimrod Wild-fire contributed, along with his break with the Jacksonians, to his defeat in the election of 1831, Though Crockett was reelected in 1833, biographers claim that his political career was also damaged by the *Sketches and Eccentricities*.[16] In 1834, he published a ghost-written autobiography to counteract the comic boisterousness of the earlier book. This *Narrative of the Life of Col. David Crockett*, though largely serious and overtly political, still contains some yarns and presents a still garrulous if less outlandish Crockett. The book went through at least seven printings in its first year. By the mid-thirties, then, when the Crockett almanacs first began to appear, the name Crockett was associated with serious writing and political activity as well as with comic sayings, heroic actions, and tall stories. The historical life and the tall tale character nourished one another and flourished into an epic cycle until finally Crockett died a heroically appropriate death at the Alamo.

Through this symbiosis of life and literature, the scantest of almanac tales gained a greater complexity simply by using the name of Crockett. The Crockett figure who fooled Mrs. Wallope in Paulding's play also conquers the Mexicans. The Crockett who wins votes by tricking a saloon keeper out of liquor for the voters receives depth and credibility from the man Crockett who really went to Congress. The sum of all these Crocketts is a symbol of cultural strengths, of common virtues exaggerated to heroic proportions, and of homely wit elaborated into art.

When the last Crockett almanac was published in 1856, the man Crockett had been dead for twenty years and the almanac writers' attempts to interest a new generation of readers had evidently failed. The *Crockett Almanac* for 1852, for example, is a ragtag miscellany of mostly third-person, non-dialect anecdotes about Daniel Boone, Mike Fink, Whaler Bill, and others; it contains nothing about Crockett.[17] When Walt Disney revived the Crockett legend in the 1950s, his mellow-voiced hero bore little resemblance to the nineteenth-century ring-tailed roarer, and there was no popular revival of interest in the Crockett almanacs. Deprived of their original personal and historical context, and lacking sufficient internal manipulation of narrative context, the almanac tales today seem to be largely extravagant jokes, with only flashes of real humor and artistry. But in 1840, the Crockett of the almanacs was a fiction based on a real man, a fantasy inspired by history, a comic hero, an inspiration for tall tales.

The Hoax

In the Crockett almanacs, language was outrageous enough, the vehicle transparent enough, and the character of the tall-talking hero familiar enough that most readers could assume the role of privileged insider in the tall tale interplay between writer and reader. Other writers, in other contexts, chose to cast the reader in the role of unsuspecting victim. Both in the early southwestern flush times and in the postwar Far West, the preferred vehicle for this victimization of the reader was the newspaper hoax. The tallest of these hoaxes report, in solemn detail, more or less incredible wonders of the western frontier, challenging the reader to detect where fact ends and imagination begins. Masquerading as a travel letter or an honest report of natural curiosities, the newspaper hoax derives from its immediate physical context the mask of factuality, the poker-faced narrative stance. The author then hints at his fictionalizing role and invites his readers to join in the humor by introducing obvious burlesque, impossible tallness, or some other self-falsifying element.

Between August 1843 and March 1844, T.B. Thorpe combined hoax, tall tale, and burlesque in a series of articles in which the author's character and relation to his material became clear only as the series progressed. Thorpe's "Letters from the Far West" pretend to be the reports of a member of Sir William Drummond Stewart's hunting party touring the northern Rockies. Printed first in Thorpe's *Concordia* (Louisiana) *Intelligencer*, the letters were picked up by other papers whose editors may or may not have believed at first in their authenticity. Simultaneously, the expedition was being reported in earnest by an actual member of the party, Matthew C. Field, who wrote for the *New Orleans Picayune* and the *St. Louis Reveille* under the pseudonym "Phazma." When after several months the *Picayune* accused the *Spirit of the Times* of a foolish gullibility for printing Thorpe's letters instead of Field's, the *Spirit's* editors roundly denied being sold and, of course, continued to print Thorpe's letters.[18]

The letters follow a form typical of travelers' correspondence — with dates, plausible place names, and even an explanation in the first number that the letter will be carried by a "half-breed" who is about to leave for "the settlements."[19] The plausible, however, quickly yields to the implausible, the ridiculous, the tall. The name "Yellow Stone," Thorpe claims, is a corruption of the Indian title "Yalhoo Stunn," which literally means "the running water with green pebbles." He further explains that he intends to introduce technical terms as much as possible in his descriptions, and then italicizes "varmints" and "calves," and in a description of an early confrontation with Indians writes "we were all expecting that a fight would come off between us and the *varlets* (technical)" (26 August 1843, p. 303). His satire of travel writing extends to those interested in natural history. In Thorpe's second letter Audubon, who actually traveled with Stewart, names a new bird *"Oxydendi-aonicuntior surimonium,* that being the classical name, he says, for a poor little feathered creature no bigger than the end of your thumb" (9 September 1843, p. 333). This bit of pseudoscience added in a postscript acts as a clue to the fantasy of the earlier descriptions and at the same time as a waggish assertion of the scientific accuracy of the entire letter. Like the oral tall tale, the newspaper hoax pretends to confirm its factuality with minute but often absurd detail.

The supposed author of the letters, "P.O.F.," describes himself as an inept greenhorn who expects buffalo to behave like cattle, tumbles from his horse, takes an involuntary ride on a bear, collects buffalo chips as curiosities, and falls victim to the incessant practical jokes of his companions. He is also the gullible victim of the old-timers' tall tales. Early in the series he reports a tall buffalo story told by an old hunter known among the Indians as "teller of truth." "So I believe it," he says. "When Matt Field heard it, he put his thumb to his nose and shook his fingers at Sir William who laughed heartily; they have already between them picked up many Indian signs which are not yet familiar to me" (23 September 1843, p. 356).

To make oneself out a fool is of course an old trick in both oral and written humor, and P.O.F., by showing himself falling for a stretcher within his own tall tale, uses self-deflating humor to point out the tallness of his reports. Using a stock motif, he describes how his wet leather clothing dried in the sun. He feels the blood rush to his head; he cannot breathe; he believes he has been poisoned. Tar-pot-wan-ja, an ignoble savage hanger-on, motions at him with a knife, while his white companions talk of pitching him into the stream. Finally released from his dangerous predicament by a good soaking in the stream, he learns that the drying, shrinking leather had choked him. An old-timer explains to him how buffaloes avoid this problem. Their shoulder humps contain fat. When the sun shines, "this fat melts, runs over the skin, and keeps water from penetrating the pores." So now P.O.F. greases his clothing every morning with buffalo grease. "And although they smell exceedingly rancid," he explains, "and compel me to associate entirely with Tar-pot-wan-ja, still I had rather do this, than endanger my life, as I have already done" (4 November 1843, p. 1).

The mask of the gullible man allows Thorpe to satirize the naïveté of the tenderfoot, but also the cruelty of the practical joker, the self-conscious machismo of the sporting gentleman, and the errors behind a romantic attitude toward the West. In his final letter he sums up what seems to be the predominant philosophy behind the "Letters":

I dreamed that the learned members of the Royal Society, London, had issued a circular, offering a thousand pounds reward for a "perpetual motion," and a display of the most foolish thing in the world; and I dreamed that I gave the society a journal of my adventures "Out West," and proved that I went out there for the purpose of "sport," and the society unanimously awarded to me the thousand pounds.   (16 March 1844, p. 33)

Predominating philosophies aside, the motivating force behind the "Letters" is humor. At least one contemporary reader took the joke properly and responded in kind. Matt Field, who appears in Thorpe's letters as a joker and a clown, finally lightened his own sober accounts of the expedition and even introduced another member of the party, the *Concordia Intelligencer* Man, who "looked like an embodiment, in semi-human form, of a thick fog on the Mississippi, at half-past three in the morning, to a man who has just lost his last dollar at poker."[20]

In Thorpe's case these fake correspondences were as much burlesque as hoax, and any real deception was meant to be brief. The open absurdity and impossible tallness of parts of the letters would suggest to even the dullest reader that something was afoot. Other hoaxes, however, are more carefully disguised, and they therefore more aggressively victimize the reader, more strenuously challenge him to perceive the tallness.

Among Mark Twain's few newspaper hoaxes, the best remembered is "The Petrified Man," published in the *Virginia City Territorial Enterprise* in 1862 and widely copied by other papers. Though solemn in tone throughout, the piece nonetheless contains a clue to its falseness:

The body was in a sitting posture, and leaning against a huge mass of croppings; the attitude was pensive, the right thumb resting against the side of the nose; the left thumb partially supported the chin, the fore-finger pressing the inner corner of the left eye and drawing it partly open; the right eye was closed, and the fingers of the right hand spread apart.[21]

In an account of his failed attempts to write hoaxes (he calls them bur-lesques), written for the *Galaxy* in 1870, Mark Twain claimed that the "Petrified Man" had been widely believed and even reprinted in the British medical journal *Lancet*.[22] The public was too well fooled, he ex-plained, because the clue was too well hidden—broken up and scat-tered among other details of the article. Though his memory may have failed him (the nose thumbing description was not so widely scattered and at least one scholar has searched in vain through the files of the *Lancet*[23]), Mark Twain has nonetheless isolated a vital attribute of the successful newspaper hoax. Where the author's intention is temporary deception, puzzlement, and finally amusement, the hoax must contain some self-revealing extravagance or self-falsifying element.[24] In Mark Twain's "Empire City Massacre" hoax, the self-falsifying clues were in-deed too well hidden among other, more compelling details. Though it described in gruesome detail the murdering spree of a man driven mad by shady mine stock dealings, the article also contained contradic-tions and errors about local characters and geography. Mark Twain had expected, he claims in the *Galaxy* article, that local readers would per-ceive the hoax, while California papers would be fooled into copying an indirect criticism of the *San Francisco Bulletin* and of "dividend-cooking" in a California mine. He misjudged his audience, however, and he allowed himself to be carried away with his imaginative gore.

[Hopkins] dashed into Carson on horseback, with his throat cut from ear to ear, and bearing in his hand a reeking scalp from which the warm, smoking blood was still dripping.[25]

The article was first believed and then vociferously condemned; Mark Twain was obliged to print a retraction.[26] With an inside audience re-stricted to the staff of the *Enterprise*, the hoax made poor copy, if only because the reputation of Mark Twain and the commercial interests of the paper demanded that a large group of readers be amused or in-formed, not shut out and deceived.

While Mark Twain finally decided that he did not care much for newspaper hoaxes anyhow and went on to other things, his cohort at the *Enterprise*, Dan DeQuille, pursued, practiced, and elaborated the

hoax far beyond anything Mark Twain had attempted. Whether or not
he really fooled anyone is, again, a matter of debate.[27] Many of his
hoaxes are transparent because of their very absurdity: a mechanical
rheumatism cure stretches a newspaper editor's legs until he is thirteen
feet six inches tall; an inventor proposes a city-wide pipeline to provide
smokers with convenient and trouble-free tobacco smoke; water from
a certain hot spring tastes exactly like chicken soup. Other hoaxes de-
emphasize the absurd and concentrate on plausible details and scientific explanations. One of the most widely circulated reported the "Sad
Fate of an Inventor":

Mr. Newhouse had constructed what he called a "solar armor," an apparatus intended to protect the wearer from the fierce heat of the sun in
crossing deserts and burning alkaline plains. The armor consisted of a
long, close-fitting jacket made of common sponge and a cap or hood of
the same material; both jacket and hood being about an inch in thickness.
Before starting across the desert, this armor was to be saturated with water.
Under the right arm was suspended an India rubber sack filled with water
and having a small gutta percha tube leading to the top of the hood. In
order to keep the armor moist, all that was necessary to be done by the
traveler as he progressed over the burning sands, was to press the sack occasionally, when a small quantity of water would be forced up and thor-
oughly saturate the hood and the jacket below it. Thus, by the evaporation
of the moisture in the armor, it was calculated might be produced any degree of cold.[28]

Unfortunately for Mr. Newhouse, the apparatus worked too well; he
as found "dead and frozen stiff" twenty miles out in Death Valley. Two
months later, DeQuille quoted an article from the *London Daily Tele-
graph* that reported the story but confessed that the editors "should
require some additional confirmation before [they] unhesitatingly accept it." DeQuille obligingly supplied further details, the result of a
supposed coroner's report, offering the more plausible explanation that
Newhouse had used not water but ether to cool his solar armor.

Like folklore, the newspaper hoax passes easily from one teller (editor, paper) to another, changing and growing as it goes along, to meet
the needs of new tellers, audiences, or circumstances. And like tall tale
folklore in particular, the newspaper hoax, through its presentation of
fiction in the garb of fact, tests the reader's recognition of the genre,
regales him with delightfully fictitious details, and offers him a sense

of identification with a select group of wits who appreciate the joke, though this group is sometimes so amorphous and invisible as to be very unlike a folk group.

The Frame Tale

If the newspaper hoax carries to the extreme involvement of the reader in a tall tale game, it does so at the expense of lasting literary popularity. Its apparent trustworthiness depends, of course, on its being found in a current paper, and the satisfaction of gradually discovering a joke comes only once. The majority of nineteenth-century tall tale writers created more self-sufficient (and therefore more lasting) works by creating more internal narrative context. Using what we now call the frame device, these writers created narrative context by re-creating tale-telling situations. In these frame tales, the implied author or frame narrator— a literate gentleman— describes in realistic detail a scene which he claims to have witnessed on a riverboat, in a storefront, or around a campfire, and sets the stage for a second narrator who then spins a tall tale. Many of these frame tales (especially in the earliest years of the flush times) seem to be close transcriptions of actual oral storytelling sessions; others are pure inventions modeled after oral sessions and earlier frame tales. The frame device allowed the writer to mimic the oral tale's social context, provided a simple method of contrasting the ordinary with the tall, and added a layer of comedy by contrasting the conventional literary voice of the frame narrator with the comic, often dialect-speaking voice of the yarnspinner. This last contrast has the potential for creating another level of tallness and pretense, for the relationships between the real author and the frame narrator, as well as between the frame narrator and the yarnspinner, may not be as they at first seem.

In many of the frame tales the narrator, called "the Self-controlled Gentleman" by Kenneth Lynn, represents a civilized moral and aesthetic norm to be contrasted with and held superior to the comedy and violence of the vernacular-speaking characters.[29] In William C. Hall's Yazoo sketches, the frame narrator's stately language and conventional morality describe "our old acquaintance, Mike Hooter": "After patronizing all the groceries, and getting rather mellow, he grew garrulous in the extreme, and forthwith began to expatiate on his wonderful exploits." Mike's own voice is characterized by dialect and tall talk. He describes the Yazoo hills as "the durndest hole that ever come along. If it ain't next place to no whar, you can take my head for er drinkin gourd . . . it comes closer bein' the jumpin off place than any I ever heard tell on."[30] Mike then spins yarns about near-fights, bear hunts, and his daughter Sal's rustic attempts at fashion.

Some frame narrators express their judgments less directly, allowing their rustics, clowns, and yarnspinners to characterize themselves through their own voices. Still the frame narrator's standards and consciousness envelop the tale. In "Where Joe Meriweather Went To," the landlady's opening monologue combines with the narrator's description to suggest that she is an uncultivated busybody:

"I do believe that's Bill Meriweather," said the old lady hostess of the 'Sign of the Buck' tavern, as, attracted by the noise of horse's hoofs, she raised her eyes from her occupation of stringing dried slips of pumpkin, and descried, this side of the first bend in the road, a traveller riding a jaded horse towards the mansion. "I do believe that's Bill Meriweather. It's about time fur him to be round agin a buyin' shoats. But whar's Joe? Phillisy Ann," continued Mrs. Harris, raising her voice, "catch a couple of young chickens, and get supper ready as soon as you can, you dratted lazy wench you, for here comes Bill Meriweather. But whar's Joe? How do you do, Mr. Meriweather?" concluded the old lady, as the stranger arrived in front of the porch.

"Lively," replied that individual, as he proceeded to dismount and tie his horse. "How do you come on yourself, old 'oman?"[31]

As soon as Bill begins to speak and the hostess to respond, we know to distance ourselves from the old lady's gullibility and to expect a tall tale. Asked how crops are out his way, Bill replies that the tobacco crops have been ruined by an animal called the Chawback. "They looks a good deal like a fox, but are as big as a three year old nigger, and can climb a tree like a squirrel." The Chawbacks steal tobacco, dry it in the tops of the pinoaks, and sit in the trees "chawing, . . . and squirtin ambeer all over the country. Got any on 'em up here yet?" "The goodness, Lord ha' mercy, no, Bill! But whar's Joe?" replies Mrs. Harris. When Bill spins a longer yarn, a variant of the traditional shrinking-leather motif, the frame narrator does nothing to inject himself into the tall tale interplay.

Other writers withdrew the frame narrator even further from the tale. "The Trapper's Story" begins simply with "'Ye see, strangers,' said the old man."[32] The author assumes that we, the readers, are there as the story is being told. Drawn in by this comfortable assumption of intimacy, we gradually discover, through the author's carefully placed clues, that the audience is composed of "Bostoners," the narrator is the famous mountaineer Black George, and we are supposed to be seated around a hunting party's campfire cooking deer meat ("Stir that fire, Ned, or this here meat wont get toasted till midnight"). Certainly by 1854 when Haliburton reprinted this tale in his anthology, and probably at the time of its first publication, the tall tale in literature was so familiar that just the mention of an old trapper and a campfire suggested an entire scene and signaled a tall tale. Only the slightest reminders of the frame narrator's presence are needed to explain the situation and to provide a literate, controlling consciousness for the reader to align himself with.

The gradual disappearance of the gentleman narrator in southwestern fiction has often been associated with the decline of the old South and failure of Whig values to create an aristocratic new South—the Clowns overtaking the Gentlemen in both life and literature. The simple formula that shows a historical shift from reliance on the Gentleman to confidence in the vernacular character is, however, inadequate. Though there was a rhetorical shift from snatches of dialect in brief sketches to entirely vernacular stories and novels, and a moral transformation from the violent half-horse, half-alligator Mike Fink to the innocent seer Huck Finn, the Self-controlled Gentleman was from the beginning open to suspicion. Even Longstreet, one of the earliest southwestern writers and (according to some) the Whig Gentleman *par excellence*, undercuts his gentleman's credibility with trite language, burlesque sentimentality, and moral ambiguity.

Here and there among the frame tales of the Flush Times we find Self-controlled Gentlemen who are in fact unreliable narrators.[33] Seeming to speak with authority, they are instead victims, fools, or tall tale yarnspinners themselves. This unreliability of the frame narrator creates the possibility of tall tale baiting and challenging between the narrator and the reader and even between the author and the reader.

T.B. Thorpe, whose bogus "Letters from the Far West" engaged readers and editors in a tall tale game of catch-me-if-you-can, created one of these suspect frame narrators in his best-known work, "The Big Bear of Arkansas," first published in the *Spirit of the Times* in 1841. A New

Englander transplanted to Louisiana because of delicate health, editor of several Whig newspapers, campaigner for Zachary Taylor, and a painter before he was a writer, an editor, or a political activist, Thorpe had sympathies with both North and South, and with both rustic vigor and Whig cultivation. His undercutting of the frame narrator is, accordingly, subtle and ambiguous, and his story's potential for victimizing readers is far less aggressive than that of genuine southerners like Longstreet or George Washington Harris. Nevertheless, the reader of "The Big Bear" may become a victim if he fails to perceive the complexities of the relationship between the frame narrator and his yarnspinner. In the end, Jim Doggett's most important characteristic is not his comic dialect but his mastery of storytelling technique and his poetic vision; and the frame narrator's essence may be not moral and artistic control but rather an ethnocentrism that blinds him to the meanings of Jim's tale.[34]

The sketch opens with a frame narrator apparently unoriginal but perhaps a bit complacent and self-important. Describing the "heterogeneous character of the passengers" on a Mississippi steamboat, he explains (with an air of self-satisfaction) that "a man of observation need not lack for amusement or instruction in such a crowd, if he will take the trouble to read the great book of character so favourably opened before him."[35] This particular man of observation writes not in vivid words of his own but in a style typical of the newspapers of his day—peppered with quotation marks and italics to set off such stock phrases and slang as a "plentiful sprinkling," "old Mississippi," the "latest paper," the "social hall," and "that *place of spirits.*" The style assures readers that this narrator—who writes and, therefore, probably thinks in conventional ways—will tell only conventional truths. Alert readers may see something more by the end.

Having established his supposed trustworthiness as an observer and analyst of men and manners, the frame narrator introduces his yarnspinner. He sees Jim Doggett primarily as a type. In the "social hall" Jim whoops and crows, then thrusts his head into the cabin, hallooing "Hurra for the Big Bar of Arkansaw!" When the narrator overhears in "a confused hum of voices . . . such broken sentences as 'horse,' 'screamer,' 'lightening is slow,' &c," the telltale "&c" reveals that the narrator sees Jim first as a representative of the "half-horse and half-alligator species of men" he mentioned in his catalog of types to be found on a Mississippi steamboat. Gradually the frame narrator and the reader discover in Jim some individuality, for we find that Jim's good natured simplicity "won the heart on sight," that his "perfect confidence in himself was irresistably droll," and that he has an answer to everything. Challenged on the point of Arkansas' perfections by a cynical Hoosier who mentions mosquitoes, Jim replies with a "knock down argument in favour of big mosquitoes":

"But mosquitoes is natur, and I never find fault with her. If they are large, Arkansaw is large, her varmints ar large, her trees ar large, her rivers ar large, and a small mosquitoe would be of no more use in Arkansaw than preaching in a cane-brake." (p. 18)

Expanding his frame beyond what is typical for such sketches, Thorpe allows Jim to banter with the other passengers, and the gentleman narrator to comment on the interchange, through more than half the sketch before finally turning it entirely over to Jim for a long, uninterrupted tale. This expanded framework allows Thorpe to demonstrate the living, shifting nature of storytelling sessions and the slipperiness of the tall tale, for Jim begins with tall talk and ends with something rather different.

Thorpe first shows Jim Doggett boasting and telling brief whoppers about Arkansas' soil, climate, and varmints, and about his role as chief hunter in this backwoods paradise. The audience's reactions vary from the nervous gullibility of a "timid little man" who seems concerned for the safety of settlers in bear country, through the curiosity of an Englishman on a hunting expedition, to the skepticism of a "'live Sucker' from Illinois, who had the daring to say that our Arkansaw friend's stories 'smelt rather tall'" (p. 22). In this casual setting—with his feet propped on the stove, with an audience ignorant of a place called Shirttail Bend and open to suggestion, belief, and doubt—Jim turns small talk into tall talk. He tells of a forty pound wild turkey, of a "good-sized sow" killed when a grain of corn shot up under her, of beets and potato hills mistaken for cedar stumps and Indian mounds, and of bears that are fat year-round.

"I recollect one perty morning in particular, of putting an old he fellow on the stretch, and considering the weight he carried, he run well. But the dogs soon tired him down, and when I came up with him wasn't he in a beautiful sweat—I might say fever; and then to see his tongue sticking out of his mouth a feet, and his sides sinking and opening like a bellows, and

his cheeks so fat he couldn't look cross. In this fix I blazed at him, and
pitch me naked into a briar patch if the steam didn't come out of the
bullet-hole ten foot in a straight line. The fellow, I reckon, was made on
the high pressure system, and the lead sort of bust his biler." (p. 20)

The tall tale conceits, the pride even in his region's defects, and the
stretching of facts to the point where they tease a listener's credulity
are the hallmarks through which Thorpe re-creates the tall tale. He
then, however, shows a change.

The gentleman frame narrator interrupts the bantering, baiting,
and tall talking by specifically requesting a tale, a "description of some
particular bear hunt." With this specific request, the informal rules of
discourse for the session have been changed, and Jim is now free to tell
a longer tale. He takes a moment, however, for a back-handed compli-
ment to the frame narrator:

He squared himself round towards me, saying, that he could give me an
idea of a bar hunt that was never beat in this world, or in any other . . .
"But in the first place, stranger, let me say, I am pleased with you, because
you ain't ashamed to gain information by asking, and listening, and that's
what I say to Countess's pups every day when I'm home; and I have got
great hopes of them ar pups, because they are continually nosing about;
and though they stick it sometimes in the wrong place they gain experience any how, and may learn something useful to boot." (p. 23)

Jim senses the condescension behind the narrator's flattery, deflates the
narrator's importance by comparing him to nosey pups, and prepares
to demonstrate his own superiority by telling a finer tale than has yet
been told. He says he will tell about a hunt "in which the greatest bar
was killed that ever lived, none excepted," because "a common hunt
would not be worth relating." Evidently a ten-foot column of steam
pouring out of a bear is to Jim a common hunt, to be passed over quickly.
What he tells now is not a simple expansion of his earlier tall material
and technique, but a long, suspenseful hunting yarn laced with both
tallness and mystery.

Though tallness and mystery may both be responses to awe, the tall
tale creates a comic order or makes some kind of comic sense out of
the awesome, inexplicable, or insufferable: the trapped man went home
and got a shovel to dig himself out, the boys' flashlights were stolen
by zitflitters, Jim's Arkansas beets and potatoes were mistaken for cedar

stumps and Indian mounds. Jim Doggett's bear story transcends the ordinary world not with comedy but with magic: the bear did not "come in like Capt. Scotts' [or Davy Crockett's] coon" because it had heard Jim Doggett was after it; it was "an unhuntable bar, an died when his time come."

The story is less a tall tale than a legend — a partly or wholly fictional story of an extraordinary or perhaps a supernatural event, told as true, serving as a lesson about the dangers and mysteries of man's life on earth. The protagonist of a legend is generally an ordinary man who is unable to control events and must, in the face of mystery, act on his merely human wisdom and initiative.[36] In Jim's legend, he and the bear are mysteriously fated for each other. "I knew the thing lived," he says, and "here was something a-purpose for me." But with his fate entangled with an unhuntable bear, Jim ceases to be the mighty hunter to whom killing bears is no more difficult than drinking, and becomes a man whose gun snaps, whose caps get lost in the lining of his coat, and who kills the wrong bear in the water. The mighty hunter is reduced to the trials of ordinary men by an extraordinary bear. But it is not a typical tall tale bear — not a bear that balances pumpkins on his head or, like the bear in "Mike Hooter's Bar Story," takes powder and flint from a gun and thumbs his nose at the hunter.[37] This is a "creation" bear, a "devil," a bear that "loom[s] up like a *black mist*," that disappears on an island, and that, in dying, groans "like a thousand sinners." The imagery is often not comical but magical.

The imagery is also earthy, and here "earthy" must be freighted with all possible richness and subtlety. In his discussion of the uses of folk imagery in Rabelais, Mikhail Bakhtin describes grotesque realism, explaining how it lowers all that is spiritual and ideal "to the material level, to the sphere of earth and body in their indissoluble unity."[38] Often this lowering is done through excretion images which, according to Bakhtin, debase at the same time that they rejuvenate, for they are mingled with and often take the place of reproductive images. Death, in grotesque imagery, is not idealized, nor is it a negation of life, but is an indispensable component of life as a whole, "the condition of its constant renewal and rejuvenation."[39] In "The Big Bear," Thorpe combines death with excretion in one of the most explicitly scatalogical scenes in nineteenth-century American literature. The morning before the planned hunt in which Jim has vowed "to catch that bar, go to

Texas, or die," Jim goes into the woods and sits down "from habit," with his "inexpressibles" down around his ankles. At that moment, the magical bear appears before him. Jim rises, aims his gun, and kills the bear. The death of the "creation" bear is thus debased, not in a pejorative sense, but in being connected with the functions of life. Once dead, the bear is no longer a mysterious force, but a source of meat and fur. Likewise Jim's accomplishment in killing the bear is degraded, but it is also enhanced, for it is, as Milton Rickels suggests, "an act of great self-possession."[40] The imagery in Jim's tale, then, probes the connection between death and regeneration, and celebrates the mystical relation between man and beast, hunter and hunted. Jim "loves [the bear] like a brother," but it is only through the bear's death that Jim can go on living in Shirt-tail Bend.

As Jim moves through tallness to mystery, the frame narrator perceives the magic in the tale and recognizes Jim's belief in it, but misses its real meaning and remains unchanged by it:

When the story was ended, our hero sat some minutes with his auditors in a grave silence; I saw there was a mystery to him connected with the bear whose death he had just related, that had evidently made a strong impression on his mind. It was also evident that there was some superstitious awe connected with the affair,—a feeling common with all "children of the wood," when they meet with any thing out of their everyday experience. He was the first one, however, to break the silence, and jumping up, he asked all present to "liquor" before going to bed,—a thing which he did, with a number of companions, evidently to his heart's content.   (p. 31)

To the frame narrator, Jim remains essentially a type—one of the "children of the wood." Untouched by the tale, the narrator then fails to respond to Jim's next social action by ignoring the invitation to drink. Legends, as well as tall tales, are intended to bind, to create common understandings of the world. In "The Big Bear," Thorpe has turned the Self-controlled Gentleman into the Self-complacent Gentleman. He is neither a standard for the values of nor a provider of security for the reader, but a narrow-visioned egotist. The reader, aware of his narrowness, enchanted by Jim's language and vision, becomes in his own right a member of Jim's audience, seated beside the Self-controlled Gentleman, not looking exclusively through his eyes.

Though Jim all along suspected the frame narrator's narrowness and condescension, he has played the tall tale game openly and told a legend in good faith, afterward offering to consolidate new friendships with a drink. In another framework story, the anonymous "The Way Billy Harris Drove the Drumfish to Market," the frame narrator is more deliberately victimized, more obviously duped. In this sketch, collected in Haliburton's 1852 anthology, although the frame narrator's voice and consciousness are kept close to the center of the tale, and although he is deficient in neither morality nor perception, he nonetheless loses a battle of wits with his vernacular yarnspinner.

He begins with only a brief sketch of the setting, but repeatedly enters to characterize the speakers and their conversation.

The afternoon of a still, sultry day, found us at the Bankhead spring, on Chaptico Bay, Maryland—Billy Harris, old "Blair," and myself. Billy was seated on the head of his canoe, leisurely discussing a bone and a slice of bread, the remnant of his mid-day's repast on the river; old "Blair" was busily engaged in overhauling and arranging the fish that he had taken in the course of the morning; while I in a state of half-listlessness, half drowsiness, was seated on the trunk of an uprooted cedar near the spring, with my head luxuriously reclining against the bank.

"Well, this is about as pooty a fish as I've had the handling ov for some time," remarked old "Blair," holding up and surveying with such satisfaction a rock about two feet and a half in length.

"Smart rock that," said Billy, as he measured the fish with his eye. "What an elegint team a couple o' dozen o' that size would make!"

"Elegint *what*, Mr. Harris?" inquired old "Blair," . . .

"Why an elegint team for a man to travel with," replied Billy. "Did I never tell you 'bout my driving the drums to the Alexandri' market?" he added, at the same time casting a furtive glance in the direction of the spot where I was seated. . . . "The fact is," said Billy, "it's a little out o' the usual run o' things, and it's not every one that I care about telling it to."[41]

The reference to a furtive glance toward the frame narrator suggests that he will play some role in the telling of the tale, but whether Billy intends him to overhear or sleep through it is not yet certain. The Billy-Blair relationship is developed first.

Billy Harris, apparently, is a white employee or underling of Mr. __, the frame narrator; and old Blair, judging from his dialect, is a Black, probably a slave. During Billy's tale about two large drum-fish that pulled his boat to market, old Blair's comments reveal his near-belief in the story, and Billy's responses suggest that old Blair's credulity urges him on to greater exaggerations. As the tales get taller, the frame narrator interrupts and, in a final comic twist, Billy coolly replies to Mr. __'s challenge to his veracity:

"Why in a little while the wind died away, and she [a little pungy] dropped behind, and I saw nothing more of her. I reckon it made the captain open his eyes, though, to see the way I crossed the bar. But the greatest expli't of all was—"

"What, you unconscionable liar—what?" exclaimed I, determined to put a stop to any further drafts upon old "Blair's" credulity.

"Why, the one you was tellin' me t'other day 'bout old Neption's hitching his sea-horses to some big island or 'nother, and pulling it up by the roots, and towing it off with the people and all on it, and anchorin' it down in some other place that he liked better," was the unexpected rejoinder.   (p. 272)

The frame narrator has risen to the bait, and Billy's tale has now achieved its true purpose. Billy has not simply astonished an old slave with an outrageous story (old Blair is probably not as naïve as his master makes him out to be, anyway); he has manipulated his gentleman employer into a ridiculous position—into calling a fiction a lie after he himself has told even more fantastic fictions. Billy has asserted that he, his language, his lifestyle, and his tall tales are at least as powerful and respect-worthy as the gentleman, his formal prose, his upper-class prudishness, and his academic fictions.

A reader who has too closely allied himself with the frame narrator finds himself in the end victimized by Billy's tale or unmoved by Jim Doggett's legend. In many a frame tale we are forced to take sides in the antagonistic confrontation between the literate frame narrator and the vernacular yarnspinner who, because they are not social equals, do not approach each other as intellectual and moral equals. By manipulating our loyalties, by changing our normal alliances, the literary tall tale enlarges our vision. We begin to perceive the moral and intellectual acuity of the uncultivated, dialect-speaking character, and we begin to appreciate the power and artistic integrity of a favorite, if somehow undignified, form of humor: the tall tale.

In one collection of frame tales, this challenge to conventionality occurs with very little framing and with no moral or intellectual degradation of the frame narrator. The narrator is neither a victim nor a patronizing observer, but an admiring accomplice to the yarnspinner, conspiring with him to challenge the reader's conception of the possible and the comic. Like Longstreet's Hall sketches, the framed yarns of George Washington Harris' *Sut Lovingood* create an aggressively tall relationship not among the characters but between author and reader. The result has been an unstable and controversial assessment of the literary value of the work.

CHAPTER 4

Sut Lovingood:
A Nat'ral Born Durn'd Yarnspinner

"Ef yu ain't fond ove the smell ove
cracklins, stay outen the kitchin."

— Sut Lovingood

Certainly they warned us—Sut, the narrator, and George Washington Harris, the author— that the Lovingood *Yarns* would, like much folk humor, be too strong to please every taste. Indeed, it has been called "the most repellent book of any merit in American literature."[1] And yet another critic has claimed that "for vivid imagination, comic plot, Rabelaisian touch, and sheer *fun*, the *Sut Lovingood Yarns* surpass anything else in American humor."[2] While almost any literary work lends itself to a variety of interpretations, criticism of the *Yarns* is peculiarly split between hilarity and disgust. The main disagreement seems to be over whether Sut's actions are so morally reprehensible as to be ineligible for humor, or whether the sensitive modern reader for some reason can, in good conscience, laugh at the discomfort, pain, and degradation that Sut describes with such relish. It may be that the nineteenth-century male readers these tales were written for, having narrower sympathies and toughened by their own hardships, laughed at pain more easily than most of us do now. Certainly some of the incidents in Harris' stories are tasteless, others grotesque, by the standards of many modern readers. I contend, however, that the radical disagreement over the value of the best of the Lovingood yarns is due more to differing perceptions of the stories' relation to the real world than to our greater squeamishness. To be fully appreciated, the *Yarns* must be understood as written versions of the tall tale.[3]

Our ability to laugh freely at discomfort generally depends upon the degree of discomfort depicted, the level of our identification with the victim, and the perceived distance between the unpleasant event and our own real world. Nearly anyone can enjoy Mark Twain's story of how William Wheeler was caught in a carpet machine and turned into fourteen yards of the best three-ply carpet.[4] But what about Mrs. Yardley being trampled by a horse? The story of Wheeler and his widow, as part of Jim Blaine's absurd monologue in *Roughing It*, is clearly a fiction and a joke. The problem with Sut's yarns is that they are not, at first glance, clearly told as fictions. Modern readers tend to consider Sut's stories to be personal narratives (which, in folk culture, call for belief), and think of him more as a practical joker than a storyteller. Yet when Harris collected the stories, which had originally been published separately in periodicals, he called the book not *The Adventures of Sut Lovingood* but *Sut Lovingood. Yarns Spun by a "Nat'ral Born Durn'd Fool."*[5] Sut is a storyteller, not simply a hell raiser who enthusiastically reports his escapades. Most of the yarns belong among the improbable tall tales: they are realistic enough to be possible, but wild enough and filled with enough ridiculous detail that the initiated listener knows not to take them as factual accounts of the narrator's experiences. Harris intends for us to understand that Sut has played some kind of a joke or gotten into a scrape; but, as with most fiction, we should concern ourselves more with the manner of the telling than with the suffering of fictional victims. The double distance established in fictional tales told by the fictional character Sut allows the reader to concentrate on the craft and the implied or symbolic meanings of the stories.

Beyond the title, our first clue to the fictionality of Sut's tales is in the non-dialect sections that frame the narratives. Each of Sut's tales is introduced by a brief non-dialect passage in which George, the frame narrator, indicates how he happened to hear Sut's yarn. Where many Southwest humorists used the framework device to provide balance, control, and assurance of a morally superior guiding intelligence, Harris uses the frame to establish that Sut's wit and verbal vitality are superior to those around him, and to indicate his position in society as a popular joker and storyteller. In "Sut Lovingood's Daddy, Acting Horse," listeners who presume to challenge his preeminence are quickly quieted by Sut's comebacks: "the rat-faced youth shut up his knife and subsided" and "The tomato-nosed man in ragged overcoat . . . went into the doggery" amidst the laughter of the crowd (pp. 20–21). Throughout the book, Sut draws to himself the center of attention as groups of men gather inside or in front of the doggery, in camp, or beside a spring.

Sut's apparent popularity and the freedom with which he roams among groups of loafers and hunters seem to belie his frequent claims of outlawry. In "Sicily Burns's Wedding," for example, Sut ends with the claim that "they is huntin' me tu kill me, I is feared" (p. 97). The severity of this statement, however, is undercut not only by Sut's own description of later encounters with wedding guests but also by the incidents in earlier stories. In "Parson John Bullen's Lizards," Parson Bullen's reward poster serves only as a vehicle and inspiration for Sut's wit — not as an inspiration for righteous bounty hunters. Finding copies of the poster "stuck up on every blacksmith shop, doggery, and store door in the Frog Mountain Range," George takes one down for preservation.

AIT ($8) Dullars REW-ARD

TENSHUN BELEVERS AND KONSTABLES! KETCH 'IM! KETCH 'IM!

This kash wil be pade in korn, ur uther projuce, tu be kolected at ur about nex camp-meetin, *ur thararter* by eny wun that ketches him, fur the karkus ove a sartin wun SUT LOVINGOOD, dead ur alive, ur ailin, an' safely giv over tu the purtectin care ove Parson John Bullin, ur lef' well tied, at Squire Mackjunkins, fur the raisin ove the devil pussonely, an' permiskusly discumfurtin the wimen very powerful, an' skeerin ove folks generly a heap, an' bustin up a promisin, big warm meetin, an' a making the wickid larf, an' wus, an' wus, insultin ove the passun orful.

Test, Jehu Wethero
Sined by me,
John Bullen, the passun.

. . . In a few days I found Sut in a good crowd in front of Capehart's Doggery, and as he seemed to be about in good tune, I read it to him.

"Yas, George, that ar dockymint am in dead yearnist sartin. Them hard shells over thar dus want me the wus kine, powerful bad. *But*, I spect ait dullers won't fetch me, nither wud ait hundred, bekase thar's nun ove 'em fas' enuf tu ketch me, nither is thar hosses by the livin jingo! Say, George, much talk 'bout this fuss up whar yu're been?' For the sake of a joke I said yes, a great deal.   (p. 49)

Sut's claims of physical danger are clearly a part of his joke and in fact belong to a popular folk genre. In her studies of tall tales and other modes of "talking trash" in the Okefenokee Swamp Rim, Kay Cothran found that, while rough practical jokes ("nonverbal lies," she calls them) really are played by country men, "much of the fun is in the later narration of the victim's plight or of the biter's being bit." She also notes that the practical joke story typically ends with a statement that the victim carries a lasting grudge.[6] Most of Sut's stories end with such a claim, and he frequently explains that he escapes from revenge only through the exercise of his long legs. From the glimpses of Sut's life provided in the framing passages we can see that these tales must be taller than life and that they are told for the fun of the telling rather than for their mimetic value.

The frames of the stories also briefly demonstrate how this tale-telling game of Sut's is to be played. In folk culture, the tall tale challenges the listener to prove himself clever or dull, in or out of the group to which the tale belongs, through his ability to recognize and appreciate the fiction. Harris' frame narrator, George, the well-educated, city-bred outsider, has become a temporary insider through his responses to Sut's tales. We get from George nothing but straight-faced reactions, no matter how outrageous the tale. He never moralizes, he never laughs, and he seldom interrupts. Other outsiders—a stranger, a schoolmaster, an encyclopedia salesman—ask stupid or impertinent questions and seem confused or offended by the moral atmosphere of Sut's tales. These listeners evoke insults and threats from Sut and are ostracized from the group, while George's solemn appreciation is rewarded by further yarns. When the old schoolmaster first interrupts Sut's "Trapping a Sheriff," and then asks George, "Is not that person slightly deranged?" George replies:

"Oh, no, not at all, he is only troubled at times with violent attacks of durn'd fool."
"He is laboring under one *now*, is he not?"
I nodded my head. "Go on, Sut."   (p. 264)

OLD BURN'S BULL RIDE

"Old Burns's Bull Ride" combines a popular motif with Sut's vivid language and raucous humor. Photograph courtesy of Cornell University Library

Only once does George crack. In "Eaves-Dropping a Lodge of Free-Masons" George begins, in somber, nostalgic tones, a story of his own boyhood adventures, only to be interrupted by Sut, who claims he will tell the tale himself, without any "durn'd nonsince, 'bout echo's an grapes, an warnit trees." As Sut reaches the climax of the tale and his imagination begins to outrun history, George protests:

"The ole man made a wicked cirklin lick at him wif his orful nakid wepun [a sword]. 'Voop,' hit went, an' cut the flat crown outen his cap, smoof es yu cud onkiver a huckleberry pie wif a case-knife."
"That part's not true, Mr. Sut," said I.
"Yes hit am, fur yu see he dun hit so slick that the crown whirl'd roun like a tin plate in the ar, six foot abuv yer hed, went faster nur yu did, an' lit afore yu, es yu flew down stars fas' es yu wer gwine. Oh, littil hoss, *he did du hit*, an' ef he'd lower'd his sites jus a scrimpshun he'd a-saved a pow'ful site ove meat an' bread frum bein wasted, an' curius pepil wud a-been now a-readin ove yur vartu's frum a lyin stone newspaper stuck in the yeath ove the graveyard yu wer a-blatherin about jus' now. (pp. 120-21)

Having been interrupted, Sut switches from the third person to the second, directly addressing George in answer to the challenge. He also changes the tone of the tale, increasing the grotesquerie and the exaggeration:

"An I haint told all, fur in yer skeer a-gwine away frum that orful place, yu run over the spot whar a fancy hous' 'bout five foot squar hed been upsot, slunged in up to yur eyebrows, amungst the slush in the hole, broke fur the krick, lunged in, onbottoned yer shut collar, dove plum thru that ar crownless cap—hit cum ofen yer heels like a hoop—swum outen yer clothes, an' jus' let every durn'd rag float away, an' then went home es nakid es a well-scraped hog, but not half es clean. The pepil what yu passed on yer way tu the krick tho't yu wer the cholery acumin, an' burn't tar in thar yards an' stuff'd ole rags onder thar doors, an' into the key-holes; an' es yu sneaked back nakid frum the krick, they tho't yu wer the ghost of a skin'd bullfrog, ur a forewarnin ove cumin famin." (p. 121)

By the end of this passage the story sounds like the tales of Sut's own misadventures. What began as a humorous anecdote about his friend's boyhood has become a tall tale: not an outrageous impossibility, but a tall tale nonetheless. That some of it stretches the facts we know from George's interruptions; that it is intended not as a serious lie but as entertainment for "the crowd" in the bar we know from George's introductory statements and Sut's asides to the audience. As in all the stories, the framing sections emphasize that these are tales told rather that actions performed.

Harris further encourages us to view the *Yarns* as tall tales by his use of traditional materials. At the beginning of "Dad's Dog School," Sut interrupts George's narration of a traditional story, insisting that only he should tell it since the incident occurred in his own family. By openly using the tall tale device of transforming traditional material into personal reminiscence, Harris and indeed Sut admit that Sut neither invented nor experienced the main events of the tale. Milton Rickels discovered that a version of this tale had been printed as an anecdote in *Yankee Notions* in 1857 on the page where "Sut Lovegood's [sic] Shirt" ended, and claims that the motif was still alive in oral tradition in the 1870s.[7] "Old Burns's Bull-Ride," in which Sicily Burns's father takes a wild ride on a bull chased by angry bees, also uses traditional material that had previously appeared in print. A story in an 1851 edition of the *Spirit of the Times* tells how Mike Fink, the riverboatman who generally triumphs in any conflict and cares little for the people in the settlements, lost a tussle with an angry bull chased by hornets, and was dropped naked in front of the Deacon's house, much to his embarrassment and the astonishment of a group of worshippers. The tale's inappropriateness to the Fink character suggests that it was a free-floating oral tale which the writer adapted to Fink to take advantage of the riverman's popularity.[8] Another of Sut's yarns, "Taurus in Lynchburg Market," is reminiscent of the early part of Fink's bull story, for both Sut and Fink find themselves holding the tail of an angry bull. (A similar motif appears in Don Lewis' story about a young camper holding a skunk's tail down, wondering what to do next.) Of course a writer may use traditional material or may imitate other writers without intending his narrator to be conscious of those sources; but at least once, in "Dad's Dog School," Sut himself draws attention to the traditional nature of his materials.

Sut also frequently adopts the traditional tall tale structural technique of beginning with realistically described events that seem probable, as well as possible, and gradually expanding the tale into the realm of the incredible. In "Hen Bailey's Reformation," even George conspires to give the story a mock air of factuality and solemnity by beginning with a tongue-in-cheek headnote:

This truthful narrative is particularly recommended to the careful consideration of the Rev. Mr. Stiggins, and his disciples, of the Brick Lane Branch of the Grand Junction Ebenezer Temperance Association. This mode of treatment can be fully relied upon. (p. 198)

Sut's story begins with a warning about drinking from gourds. The action of the tale then moves from Hen's mistakenly drinking turpentine to his swallowing an eight-inch lizard that had hidden in a drinking gourd, and on through his desperate acrobatics as he tries vainly to get the lizard up. Finally, when a mole sent up his trouser leg comes out his mouth on the tail of the scurrying lizard, we know we have been sold.

Once we are alert to them, tall tale characteristics abound in the *Yarns*. Sut maintains strictly his pose of truthfulness and plausibility when George attempts to catch him off guard. How did the quilting turn out? George asks, and Sut replies, "How the hell du yu 'speck me tu know? I warn't thar eny more" (p. 148). When he can get away with it, however, Sut inserts the knowledge of an omniscient narrator into otherwise first-person accounts of his adventures. In "Assisting at a Negro Night-Meeting," for example, Sut tells George what the preachers were thinking:

The suckit rider tuk hit [a beef bladder filled with "carburated hydorgen"] tu be the breast ove a fat roas hen, an the Baptis thot hit wer the bulge ove a jug. (p. 161)

And in "Old Burns's Bull Ride" Sut gives a detailed account of Burns's adventure without explaining how he happens to know the details when he had already "put the mountain atwixt" himself and the Burns's "plantashun" (96).

Mixed with this mock-historical accuracy is a good deal of tall tale exaggeration. Describing his mother's encounter with a sand-hill crane, Sut claims that she "outrun her shadder thuty yards in cummin half a mile" (p. 68). In " Dad's Dog School," the pretended factuality of a folk tale is undercut by similar exaggeration. In an attempt to convey the grotesque proportions of the Squire's nose, Sut claims that once "a feller broke a dorg-wood hanspike ur a chesnut fence rail, I'se forgot which, acrost that nose, an' twenty-seven bats, an' three kingfishers flew outen hit" (p. 287). Sut's uncertainty about the exact weapon used on the Squire's nose typifies a tall tale technique in which humor arises from the conjunction of gross exaggeration and a pretended concern for historical accuracy. Minute absurd details also characterize the tall tale, and Harris sprinkles these about the yarns as well:

[Sut's dad] seemed to run jis adzactly as fas' es a ho'net cud fly; hit were the titest race I ever seed, fur wun hoss to git all the whippin. Down thru a saige field they all went, the ho'nets makin hit look like thar were smoke roun' dad's bald hed, an' he wif nuffin on the green yeath in the way ove close about im, but the bridil, an' ni ontu a yard ove plow line sailin behine, wif a tir'd out ho'net ridin on the pint ove hit.   (p. 25)

Such precise detail simultaneously brings these exaggerations to life and points out that they are fictions.

While some of the tales contain only one or two clues to their tallness, many obvious tall tale characteristics appear in one of Harris' most popular tales—"Sicily Burns's Wedding." Perhaps it is because so many clues are given that most modern readers can recognize the story as a *story* and thus comfortably enjoy the humor. In this yarn, folkloric sources are suggested by the bull-ride motif. Harris also prepares the reader for a tall tale by first allowing Sut a straight-faced comic monologue on several topics having little to do with the story he eventually tells. Like the storytellers Mark Twain describes in "How to Tell a Story," Sut "strings incongruities and absurdities together" as if they were utterly serious and important.

I'll jus' gin yu leave tu go tu the devil ha'f hamon, if I didn't make fewer tracks tu the mile, an' more to the minit, than were ever made by eny human body, since Bark Wilson beat the saw-log frum the top ove the Frog Mountain intu the Oconee River, an dove, an' dodged hit at las'. I hes allers look'd ontu that performince of Bark's as onekel'd in histery, allers givin way to dad's hon'et race, however.

"George, every livin thing hes hits pint, a pint ove sum sort. Ole Bullen's pint is a durn'ed fust rate, three bladed, dubbil barril'd, warterproof hypockracy, an' a never-tirein appertite fur bal'face [liquor]. Sicily Burns's pint am tu drive men folks plum crazy, an' then bring em too agin. Gin em a rale Orleans fever in five minits, an' then in five minits more, gin them a Floridy ager. Durn her, she's down on her heels flatfooted now. Dad's pint is tu be king ove all durn'd fools, ever since the day ove that feller what cribb'd up so much co'n down in Yegipt, long time ago, (he run outen his coat yu minds). The Bibil tells us hu wer the stronges' man—hu wer the bes' man—hu wer the meekis man, an' hu wer the wises' man, but leaves yu to guess hu wer the bigges' fool. . . ."   (pp. 87-88)

As the real action of the story begins, Sut liberally tosses in absurd details typical of the tall tale. The bee-covered bull, for example, backs into a tall Dutch clock, "bustin' hits runnin geer outen hit, the little wheels a-trundlin over the floor, an the bees even chasin them" (p. 92). Sut also assigns to the bees the kind of exaggerated malice and intellect that most tall tale insects seem to possess: "they am pow'ful quick tempered littil critters, enyhow. The air wer dark wif 'em, an' Sock were kivered all over, from snout tu tail, so clost yu cudent a-sot down a grain ove wheat fur bees, an' they wer a-fiting one anuther in the air, fur a place on the bull" (p. 91). Because the tall language draws attention to itself and away from the distress of bull and humans, the net effect is comic. Sut also employs understatements which are reminiscent of oral tall tales. After describing the wedding guests' frantic attempts to escape the bees, Sut remarks, "liveliest folks I ever did see" (p. 95). In a more extended use of comic understatement, Sut praises old Burns' skill with a basket: "I swar old Burns kin beat eny man on top ove the yeath a-fiting bees wif a baskit. Jis set 'im a-straddil ove a mad bull, an let thar be bees enuf tu exhite the ole man, an' the man what beats him kin break me" (p. 94).

The tall tale is also, of course, suggested by the near-impossibility of some of the story's main events: the bull piling all the tables on top of one another, with Mrs. Clapshaw perched on top of the pile; old Burns being thrown onto the bull's back and later (in the sequel, "Old Burns's Bull Ride") thrown off and caught in a tree, dangling by his heels. Quite possible but clearly a stretcher is Sut's claim that "they is huntin' me tu kill me, I is fear'd"(p. 97).

At the end of the wedding story, Sut slips quickly into more general remarks and a lament on his foolishness:

"Hit am an orful thing, George, tu be a nat'ral born durn'd fool. Yu'se never 'sperienced hit pussonally, hev yu? Hits made pow'fully agin our famerly, an all owin tu dad. . . ."   (p. 97)

Like many tall tale narrators, in order to lend an air of credibility to his story and maintain a facade of seriousness, Sut ends not with a punch line but with a solemn statement about the significance of the action or with a transition to another topic of conversation.

Each of Sut's stories contains such tall tale elements, though the tallness is not equally obvious in all of the tales. In the collected *Yarns*, the better tales provide a guide for reading the lesser ones, and the book as a whole can be read as a collection of tall tales. Probably Sut is a rough joker; perhaps he does get into scrapes and live in an under-civilized world. But in his tales, these exaggerated or invented accounts of his escapades, the reader is intended to laugh not so much at the discomfiture of Sut's victims, but at his vivid comic language and at the outrageous, exaggerated relation between cause and effect, action and reaction. The initiated reader delights in seeing those exaggerated events illuminated by Sut's pyrotechnic language, and he feels liberated by the wild comic disorder at the same time that he admires Sut's imposition of artistic control on a disorderly world.

In creating this comic disorder, in flaunting and exaggerating his defects of sense and morality, Sut plays the role of the professional buffoon of literature and folklore, described by Enid Welsford as "an absurd ne'er-do-well . . . who earns his living by an openly acknowledged failure to attain to the normal standard of human dignity."[9] Unlike the court fool, who is mentally deranged, often physically deformed, and utterly dependent upon his patrons, and unlike the ordinary rogue (America's Confidence Man), who makes his living by deceiving others, professional buffoons "have gained some kind of recognition for themselves as men whose acknowledged defects are socially acceptable as a source of entertainment."[10] In folk society, this position may be filled by a local yarnspinner, as it was in the Okefenokee Swamp Rim society studied by Kay Cothran.

The storyteller is a source of pride for his locality. . . . But the man of words may also be a liability, because the social stratum from which he comes is an embarrassing one to the middle class. . . . Story tellers are headstrong men, deviant but clever or normal enough to stay out of jail and asylum, undersocialized but not unacceptably more than the common run of men, accomplished fantasists from a moribund society of fantasy makers, anarchs in terms of middle class law-oriented society.[11]

While Sut's defects of sense and morality place him at the fringes of what a man can do and still stay out of jail or asylum, his eccentricity also makes him useful and entertaining to men more conforming than he. Scorned as a sinner by the righteous, cursed as a troublemaker by the respectable, and rebuffed as a clown by the beautiful Sicily Burns, Sut remains ever popular as a hunting and drinking companion. Even his social superiors solicit his company and encourage his tales and pranks, as he demonstrates in "The Snake-Bit Irishman." In that story, "some three ur four clever fellers frum Knoxville" invite Sut along on a hunting trip, and then offer him a pair of new boots if he will scare off a vagabond Irishman who has joined them. Sut drives the man off by making him believe he is being attacked by snakes. Within the tale, Sut's prank satisfies his companions, while the telling of the tale amuses George, who is of course the best example of the socially normal man enjoying the company of the socially deviant buffoon. Unwilling to deviate openly from cultural values and the normal standards of human dignity, the socially normal characters and readers vicariously enjoy Sut's freedom. Enid Welsford's assessment of the appeal of Til Eulenspiegel applies equally to Sut Lovingood:

To identify oneself with Eulenspiegel is to feel for a moment invulnerable. True, one must regard other men as puppets of sawdust [in Sut's world, animals or machines], but then identification with Eulenspiegel does, for the time being, delude one into the intoxicating fancy that other men *are* made of sawdust, that sensation is not real, that fact is not inexorable, and that pain itself is comic. This momentary relief from the pressure of sympathy and fear is surely one of the secrets of comedy.[12]

We can enjoy Sut's crudeness, sensuality and vengeance at a safe distance — behind the facade of laughter and, furthermore, behind the buffer of fiction; for Sut, unlike Eulenspiegel, is not just a prankster but a storyteller.

Because he tells tall tales, Sut's pranks and social defects are not limited to the realm of the possible and the likely, and he uses this freedom deliberately to manipulate his audience. As he exaggerates the grotesqueness of his adventures and pushes on the limits of our credibility, he also approaches the limits of our ability to believe that other men are animals or machines and that pain is comic. Sut's yarns, then, offer the typical tall tale challenge: enjoy these tall tales and be, for the time at least, one of the boys (a society of free spirits) or be offended by them and be, like the schoolmaster and encyclopedia salesman, an outsider and an effete social conformist. The naïve, overly squeamish listener (or reader) aligns himself with the victims of Sut's social aggression: Clapshaw, Sheriff Doltin, Parson Bullen, Mrs. Yardley. True, Sut sometimes victimizes the downtrodden and innocent as well as the socially smug. He disrupts a Negro camp meeting, terrorizes an Irish tramp, torments a turpentine-poisoned drunk, and kills or maims several animals. Nontheless, these are tall tales, and the listeners or readers who fail to recognize them as such and grant an undue amount of pity to the imaginary victims become victims themselves: first, because they have identified themselves with the squeamish middle-class hypocrites of Sut's tales; second, because they suffer the discomforts of being offended rather than being entertained or relieved of psychic pressures; and, finally, because they have been fooled into believing a fiction.

While giving Sut a kind of immediate power over his listeners and readers, his yarns also give him power over the world he lives in. The absurdity of that world, not entirely generated by Sut's pranks and not entirely imaginary, impinges on Sut as well as on the other characters. As a means of coping with the stupidity of his father, the temptations of Sicily Burns, the interferences of the clergy, the hypocrisy of the middle class, and the general disorder around him, Sut creates tales which accentuate these stresses. In tales like "Parson John Bullen's Lizards" and "Trapping a Sheriff," Sut's triumph is obvious. The prank brings pain and humiliation to the victim, the story's form and context allow Sut to exaggerate his success, and the comic tone brings further humiliation as the victim becomes the butt of a humorous tale. In tales where Sut himself is the victim ("Sut's New Fangled Shirt," "Blown up with Soda," "Taurus in Lynchburg Market") and in the tales where Sut's primary function is merely to observe and report the workings of an unruly world ("Sut Lovingood's Daddy, Acting Horse," "A Razor-Grinder in a Thunder-Storm," "Bart Davis's Dance," "Dad's Dog School"), Sut masters his world by re-creating it in his own image. Sut the tall tale artist controls his fictional world more surely than Sut the prankster could ever hope to control the real world. Even the affliction of Sut's own durn'd fooledness can be mitigated through storytelling:

"Why, Sut, what's wrong now? you look sick."

"Heaps wrong, durn my skin—no my haslets—ef I haint mos' ded, an' my looks don't lie when they hints I'se sick. I is sick—I'se skin'd."

"Who skinned you—old Bullen?"

"No, hoss, a durnder fool nor Bullen did hit; I jis skin'd mysef."

"What in the name of common sense did you do it for?"

"Didn't du hit in the name ove common sense; did hit in the name, an' wif the sperit, ove plum natral born durn fool.

"Lite ofen that ar hoss, an' take a ho'n; I wants two ove 'em, (shaking his constant companion, a whiskey flask, at me,) an' plant yersef ontu that ar log, an' I'll tell ef I kin, but hit's a'mos beyant tellin.

"I'se a durnder fool nor enybody outside a Assalum, ur Kongriss, 'sceptin ove my own dad, fur he actid hoss, an' I haint tried that yet."   (p. 30)

Then follows the story of how Sut became stuck inside a freshly starched shirt and lost a good deal of his hide in getting out of it. He ends with this warning:

"Now George, ef a red-heded 'oman wif a reel foot axes yu to marry her, yu *may* du hit; ef an 'oman wants yu tu kill her husban, yu *may* du hit; ef a gal axes yu tu rob the bank, an' take her tu Californy, yu *may* du hit; ef wun on em wants yu tu quit whisky, yu *mout* even du that. But ef ever an 'oman, ole ur yung, purty es a sunflower ur ugly es a skin'd hoss, offers yu a shut aninted wif paste tu put on, jis' yu kill her in her tracks, an' burn the cussed pisnus shut rite thar. Take a ho'n?"   (p. 36)

In orthodox tall tale style and spirit, Sut exaggerates life's difficulties and conquers them by laughing at them.

Behind the character Sut is George Washington Harris exaggerating, laughing, and conquering as he spins tall tales for his readers. In Sut Lovingood, Harris exaggerated the common notion of a poor white southern mountaineer much as, in oral lore, a farmer may exaggerate the poverty of his land, the appetite of the local insects, and the ferocity of the weather for the benefit of the tourist. Harris' use of Sut as a narrator for his anti-Lincoln pieces indicates just whom Harris was trying to offend, fool, and exclude, and whom he intended to amuse. He had begun writing political articles in 1839 and was active in secessionist politics through the fifties. The first of his Sut stories, "Sut Lovingood's Daddy, Acting Horse," appeared in the *Spirit of the Times* in 1854, but thereafter the yarns were published in Democratic newspapers of the South. Though the book *Sut Lovingood* was published in New York in 1867, the Lincoln pieces and other obvious satires were not included.

For Harris, Sut is a regional characteristic to be flaunted, a weapon to be wielded. Sut represents the lowest elements of southern culture — the white trash whose shiftlessness, sexual promiscuity, cruelty to the

Negro, personal filth, and disrespect for the laws and values of Christian civilization would have chilled the very bones of any Yankee who met him. In the Sut Lovingood pieces, Harris the Southerner fought the battle against the North, industrial society, and the Republican party, not with the romantic agrarianism of a John Pendleton Kennedy or a John Esten Cooke, but with the aggressive humor of the tall tale. Even so, like all tall tales, these stories are primarily humorous, and Harris, like Sut, must have taken a great deal of delight in telling his *Yarns*.

CHAPTER 5

Mark Twain:
Roughing it on a Tall Frontier

I confiscated [the name MARK TWAIN] from Captain Sellers,
and have done my best to make it remain what it was in his
hands—a sign and symbol and warrant that whatever is found in
its company may be gambled on as being the petrified truth.
How I've succeeded, it would not be modest for me to say.
                                        —*Life on the Mississippi*

The narrator of *Roughing It* is neither the illiterate roughneck of the
southwestern humorous tradition nor the polite, highly civilized frame
narrator who presented that roughneck for the reading public's inspec-
tion. He is Mark Twain, the American Vandal—garrulous and irreverent but not illiterate; familiar with hard work and rough living but also
with the culture of Boston and of Europe; comic, boastful, and self-
deprecating; and, above all, proud of being an American.

By the time Samuel Langhorne Clemens published *Roughing It*, in
1872, his readers were well acquainted with Mark Twain. Following him
through Europe and the Holy Land in *The Innocents Abroad*, they had
joined him in comic defiance of the Old World's supposed cultural superiority. The Innocent vandalized Europe with his irreverence and
skepticism, by laughing in the presence of its relics. In *Roughing It*,
once tentatively titled *The Innocents at Home*, the reader and author
join in a celebration of the great American West and discover the origin
of the American Vandal. In the transformation from the false dignity
of the literary gentleman to the exuberant humor and irreverence of
the Vandal, the transforming agent is the American frontier.

In his platform lectures on the *Innocents Abroad* material, Mark

Twain used the term American Vandal to describe "the roving, independent, free and easy character of that class of travelling Americans who
are *not* elaborately educated, cultivated and refined, and gilded and
filigreed with the ineffable graces of the first society." Far from trying
to imitate European gentility, the Vandal is proud of his American
plainness and forthrightness. "He is always self possessed, always untouched, unabashed — even in the presence of the Sphinx."[1] To be unabashed in the presence of kings and queens and the Sphinx, to view
a bust of Columbus and ask, in order to befuddle the effusive tour
guide, "Is he dead?" and to make light of Moses' forty years in the
wilderness, one must, according to Mark Twain, be an American.

Roughing It, written after *The Innocents Abroad* but describing an
earlier period in the narrator's life, exhibits the creation of an irreverent,
yarnspinning American Vandal. The book itself is a tall tale which presents a series of adventures, disillusionments, wonders, and plain facts
that formed the character of the narrator and created in him the tall
tale state of mind.

The tall tale state of mind is skeptical, irreverent, defiant. Just as
the characters in *The Innocents Abroad* recognized the squalor of the
Holy Land and refused to go into ecstasies over dim paintings by the
old masters, so the narrator of *Roughing It* sees dirt and degradation
in place of noble savages, describes a buffalo hunt with humor rather
than sentimental admiration, and confesses the toil and tedium of mining silver and gold. The tale teller also possesses an energetic imagination which evokes the bizarre possibilities of a tall world — in this case
a world of deserts and floods, destitute miners and millionaires, silver and fool's gold, sage-brush and mountain peaks. Finally, the tall
tale state of mind tries to cope with fear, social conflict, natural disaster, and even general cosmic chaos by exaggerating them to comic
proportions.

From the beginning, the narrator's distinctive voice echoes and en-
compasses change, by yoking the perspective of the experienced narrator with the naïve illusions of his tenderfoot days:

My brother had just been appointed Secretary of Nevada Territory. . . . I
was young and ignorant, and I envied my brother. I coveted his distinction
and his financial splendor, but particularly and especially the long, strange
journey he was going to make, and the curious new world he was going to
explore. He was going to travel! I never had been away from home, and
that word "travel" had a seductive charm for me. Pretty soon he would be

hundreds and hundreds of miles away on the great plains and deserts, and among the mountains of the Far West, and would see buffaloes and Indians, and prairie dogs, and antelopes, and have all kinds of adventures, and may be get hanged or scalped, and have ever such a fine time, and write home and tell us all about it, and be a hero. And he would see the gold mines and the silver mines, and maybe go about of an afternoon when his work was done, and pick up two or three pails of shining slugs, and nuggets of gold and silver on the hillside.[2]

The telltale string of absurdities in this passage suggests a poker-faced narrator who may or may not be precisely describing his former attitudes and beliefs, but who, at any rate, clearly scorns the wide-eyed romantic he claims once to have been, and who would like to amuse us with the story of his education. His present perspective and attitudes are revealed in an early discussion of the sage-brush campfire. "It makes a very sociable camp-fire," he explains, "and one around which the most impossible reminiscences sound plausible, instructive, and profoundly entertaining" (p. 55). Then follows an example.

Mark Twain doesn't announce the tall tale any more than a folk raconteur would. In classic tall tale form, he leads casually into the story via a discussion of the eating habits of the jackass and the mule. This leads him to the voraciousness of the camel:

In Syria, once, at the head-waters of the Jordon, a camel took charge of my overcoat while the tents were being pitched, and examined it with a critical eye, all over, with as much interest as if he had an idea of getting one made like it; and then, after he was done figuring on it as an article of apparel, he began to contemplate it as an article of diet. He put his foot on it, and lifted one of the sleeves out with his teeth, and chewed and chewed at it, gradually taking it in, and all the while opening and closing his eyes in a kind of religious ecstasy, as if he had never tasted anything as good as an overcoat before, in his life. Then he smacked his lips once or twice, and reached after the other sleeve. Next he tried the velvet collar, and smiled a smile of such contentment that it was plain to see that he regarded that as the daintiest thing about an overcoat. The tails went next, along with some percussion caps and cough candy, and some fig-paste from Constantinople. And then my newspaper correspondence dropped out, and he took a chance in that—manuscript letters written for the home papers. But he was treading on dangerous ground, now. He began to come across solid wisdom in those documents that was rather weighty on his stomach; and occasionally he would take a joke that would shake him up till it loosened his teeth; it was getting to be perilous times with him, but he held his grip with good courage and hopefully, till at last he began to stumble on statements that not even a camel could swallow with impunity. He began to gag and gasp, and his eyes to stand out, and his forelegs to spread, and in about a quarter of a minute he fell over as stiff as a carpenter's work-bench, and died a death of indescribable agony. I went and pulled the manuscript out of his mouth, and found that the sensitive creature had choked to death on one of the mildest and gentlest statements of fact that I ever laid before a trusting public.

I was about to say, when diverted from my subject, that occasionally one finds sage-brushes five or six feet high, and with a spread of branch and foliage in proportion, but two or two and a half feet is the usual height.   (pp. 55–56)

Beyond being, as Mark Twain says, "profoundly entertaining," this passage does several things. First, it suggests that the narrator is our friend the Vandal, who traveled to Syria in *The Innocents Abroad*. Secondly, rather than merely informing the reader about "impossible reminiscences," it allows him partly to experience the tall tale—to be drawn innocent and unaware from the world of fact to a world of comic, exaggerated fiction and then to be brought back to the real world without explanation or apology. Finally, the story serves as a warning that this narrator will not always write plain facts; his mild and gentle statements of fact are apt to be largely exaggerated and peculiarly humorous.

With this present persona established, Mark Twain moves on to spin the tale of his transformation. The naïve youth becomes a teller of tall tales by experiencing the strangeness of events on the frontier, the magnificence of nature in the West, and the inevitable tensions between dissimilar groups of people on the fringes of society.[3]

The strange and surprising things that happen on the frontier induce in the newcomer both an attitude of irreverence toward his former beliefs and a tendency to exaggerate present or past adventures. When the "noble sport" of buffalo hunting, begun by "galloping over the plain in the dewy freshness of the morning" ends with George Bemis being chased two miles by a wounded buffalo bull, the result is a tall tale. Bemis, humiliated by his ordeal, suffers in silence for twenty-four hours and then produces a yarn which transforms his defeat into a comic victory. Having been thrown from his terrified horse, Bemis climbs "the

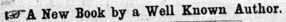

A New Book by a Well Known Author.

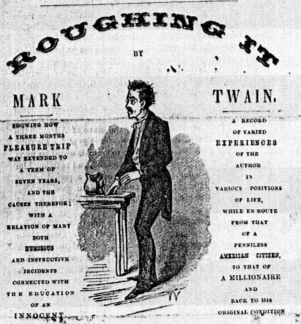

The publisher's announcement for *Roughing It* draws on Mark Twain's
reputation both as a lecturer and as the author of *The Innocents Abroad*.
The book itself does indeed depict "the education of an innocent."
Photograph courtesy of the Henry W. and Albert A. Berg Collection.
The New York Public Library. Astor, Lenox and Tilden Foundations.

only solitary tree there was in nine counties adjacent" and prepares for the worst:

"Sure enough, it was just as I had dreaded, he started in to climb the tree. . . . Up he came—an inch at a time—with his eyes hot, and his tongue hanging out. Higher and higher—hitched his foot over the stump of a limb, and looked up, as much as to say, 'You are my meat, friend.' Up again—higher and higher, and getting more excited the closer he got. He was within ten feet of me! I took a long breath,—and then said I, 'It is now or never.' I had the coil of the lariat all ready; I paid it out slowly, till it hung right over his head; all of a sudden I let go of the slack, and the slip-noose fell fairly round his neck! Quicker than lightning I out with the Allen [revolver] and let him have it in the face. It was an awful roar, and must have scared the bull out of his senses. When the smoke cleared away, there he was, dangling in the air, twenty foot from the ground, and going out of one convulsion into another faster than you could count! I didn't stop to count, anyhow—I shinned down the tree and shot for home."
    "Bemis, is all that true, just as you have stated it?"
    "I wish I may rot in my tracks and die the death of a dog if it isn't."   (Chapter VII)

Bemis has deceived no one with this extravagant tale, but the telling of the tale exorcises his anger and humiliation and reintegrates him with his companions.

    Mark Twain immediately follows Bemis' tale with an anecdote from an imaginary visit to Bangkok. He tells of Eckert, "a person famous for the number, ingenuity and imposing magnitude of his lies" and Bascom, "an influential man, and a proud and sometimes irascible man" who boasts that he can lure Eckert into telling a specimen lie. Eckert, however, knows he is being baited. He makes an unlikely claim about a cat that will eat coconut; but the "sell" in this instance consists of telling a truth that looks like a lie, for the cat does indeed eat coconut. Bascom, defeated, asks the narrator not to mention this incident to "the boys." By itself, this anecdote demonstrates how tall tales and practical jokes can be used to reduce a swollen ego. Placed as it is, immediately following Bemis' buffalo story, it also demonstrates that one should not overestimate his ability to tell fact from fiction.

    The next two chapters recapitulate this theme. First, Mark Twain explains the remarkable achievement of the pony express, which carried mail nineteen hundred miles in eight days, and describes the difficult, dangerous regimen of horse and rider. When finally the narrator sees a pony rider, his amazement verges on disbelief:

So sudden is it all, and so like a flash of unreal fancy, that but for the flake of white foam left quivering and perishing on a mail sack after the vision had flashed by and disappeared, we might have doubted whether we had seen any actual horse and man at all, maybe.   (p. 84)

The wonderful pony express actually existed, but the remainder of the chapter continues to question the wonders of the West. The narrator ridicules himself for being "complacent and conceited" about having seen things that other people had not, as if simply seeing them raised his own worth; he summarizes tall tales told about an Indian mail robbery and massacre; and he reports but does not verify "the most trustworthy tradition" about the ordeal of a lone survivor of that massacre.[4]

Chapter IX continues the exploration of tall facts by describing a stage ride through dangerous Indian country and the midnight murder of a stage driver. Although the narrator explains that they "never did get much satisfaction about that dark occurrence," he seems not to doubt that the man was actually murdered. The supposed dead man, however, was not a particularly reliable character. He had once told them that on an earlier, more southern route that took the stage among the Apaches, the Indians "used to annoy him all the time . . . and that he came as near as anything to starving to death in the midst of abundance, because they kept him so leaky with bullet holes that he 'couldn't hold his vittles'" (p. 87). Have the passengers been the victims of a midnight hoax instigated by this yarnspinning stage driver, or has the driver really been murdered by outlaws at a stage station, leaving the conductor and the new driver unconcerned? The narrator does not overtly raise this question, but the context suggests it. The next two chapters support the notion that this midnight adventure might very well have been a murder and not a hoax, for they present the remarkable history of Slade—"the most bloody, the most dangerous and the most valuable citizen that inhabited the savage fastnesses of the mountains" (p. 90). The alert reader, however, has by this time learned that the boundary between tall tale and tall fact is often indistinguishable.

The extraordinary experiences of miners also nourish a tall tale frame of mind. The original owners of the Gould and Curry claim lost a fortune by selling out too early:

Mr. Curry owned two thirds of it—and he said that he sold it out for twenty-five hundred dollars in cash, and an old plug horse that ate up his market value in hay and barley in seventeen days by the watch. And he said that Gould sold out for a pair of second-hand government blankets and a bottle of whiskey that killed nine men in three hours, and that an unoffending stranger that smelt the cork was disabled for life. Four years afterward the mine thus disposed of was worth in the San Francisco market seven millions six hundred thousand dollars in gold coin.   (p. 291)

The tall tale's absurd contrast enlivens and emphasizes the magnitude of the loss, and at the same time allows Curry to console himself with laughter.

The transformation from tenderfoot to seasoned yarnspinner also results from the tensions between dissimilar groups of people on the frontier. When the narrator makes a stop in Utah, he first experiences the severe psychological tension created by contact with people of radically different values and experiences. His fascination with Mormon polygamy combines curiosity, amusement, and moral indignation. Such a strong mixture, apparently shared by the Gentile residents of Salt Lake City, yields an outrageous story, purportedly told by a man named Johnson, about Brigham Young's troubles with his dozens of wives and hundreds of children.

"Bless my soul, you don't know anything about married life. It is a perfect dog's life, sir—a perfect dog's life. You can't economize. It isn't possible. . . . Think of the wash bill—(excuse these tears)—nine hundred and eighty four pieces a week. No, sir, there is no such thing as economy in a family like mine. Why just the one item of cradles—think of it! And vermifuge! Soothing syrup! Teething rings! . . . Bless you, sir, at a time when I had seventy-two wives in this house, I groaned under the pressure of keeping thousands of dollars tied up in seventy-two bedsteads when the money ought to have been out at interest; and I just sold out the whole stock, sir, at a sacrifice, and built a bedstead seven feet long and ninety-six feet wide. But it was a failure, sir. I could *not* sleep. It appeared to me that the whole seventy-two women snored at once. The roar was deafening. And then the danger of it! That was what I was looking at. They would all draw in their breath at once, and you could actually see the walls of the house suck in—and then they would all exhale their breath at once, and you could see the walls swell out, and strain, and hear the rafters crack, and the shingles grind together." (pp. 125–26)

Though he provides many facts about the government, economy, and society of Utah, the narrator admits that the two days spent there were not enough to "settle the 'Mormon question.'" The fantastic tale about Brigham Young's domestic difficulties reveals not the truth about polygamy or Mormonism, but the truth about the Gentiles' attitude toward the Mormons.

At the conclusion of the Utah section, Mark Twain discusses the embarrassments of being an immigrant among old-timers—being unaccustomed to high prices for trivial articles, having a white shirt, and being unable to "swear in the presence of ladies without looking the other way" (p. 138). Again a tale helps him to cope with the discomfort. Ignorantly underpaying "a young half-breed" boot-black, the narrator is rebuked before an audience of mountaineers, teamsters, and stage drivers.

Presently [the boot-black] handed the half dime back to me and told me I ought to keep my money in my pocket-book instead of in my soul, and then I wouldn't get it cramped and shriveled up so!
    What a roar of vulgar laughter there was! I destroyed the mongrel reptile on the spot, but I smiled all the time I was detaching his scalp, for the remark he made *was* good for an "Injun." (p. 138)

By exaggerating and making light of the episode, the narrator attempts to salvage some dignity from the humiliation of being a newcomer. He also aligns himself with the witnesses by forcing the boot-black into the role of outsider.

Great differences in knowledge and values also inspire the tall tale's practical manifestation, the hoax. "The older citizens of a new territory," according to Mark Twain, "look down upon the rest of the world with a calm, benevolent compassion, as long as it keeps out of the way—when it gets in the way they snub it" (p. 224). In the Great Landslide hoax, most of the population of Carson City elaborately snubbed a self-important newcomer, General Buncombe, who considered himself "a lawyer of parts." One day Dick Hyde rode furiously up to the general's door and asked him to bring suit against Tom Morgan, whose entire ranch had come tumbling down the mountain in a landslide, coming to rest atop Hyde's ranch. Morgan, it seems, now claimed ownership of the spot that used to belong to his neighbor. Hyde's description of the landslide should have alerted Buncombe to the joke:

He had the infernal meanness to ask me why didn't I *stay* on my ranch and hold possession when I see him a-coming! Why didn't I *stay* on it, the blathering lunatic — by George, when I heard that racket and looked up that hill it was like the whole world was a-ripping and a-tearing down that mountain side — splinters, and cordwood, thunder and lightning, hail and snow, odds and ends of hay stacks, and awful clouds of dust! — trees going end over end in the air, rocks as big as a house jumping 'bout a thousand feet high and busting into ten million pieces, cattle turned inside out and a-coming head on with their tails hanging out between their teeth! — and in the midst of all that wrack and destruction sot that cussed Morgan on his gate-post a-wondering why I didn't *stay and hold possession*! Laws bless me, I just took one glimpse, General, and lit out'n the county in three jumps exactly.   (p. 225)

Preoccupied with his intellectual sophistication and legal expertise, General Buncombe is an easy victim for the tough old-timers who have seen real landslides and who have their own code for determining property rights. The hoax attempts to cure Buncombe of his pride; the story told about it afterward serves as an example and warning to other newcomers and to readers who may not yet be convinced that on the frontier men in white shirts are the ones to be pitied.

The initiation stories which the narrator tells on himself further demonstrate the evolution of the tall tale state of mind. When he resolves to buy a horse, Mark Twain learns something about horses; but, more importantly, he learns that appearance may belie the facts and a straight face may conceal a deception:

A man whom I did not know (he turned out to be the auctioneer's brother) noticed the wistful look in my eye, and observed that that was a very remarkable horse to be going at such a price; and added that the saddle alone was worth the money. . . .

"I know that horse — know him well. You are a stranger, I take it, and so you might think he was an American horse, maybe, but I assure you he is not. He is nothing of the kind; but — excuse my speaking in a low voice, other people being near — he is, without the shadow of a doubt, a Genuine Mexican Plug!"

I did not know what a Genuine Mexican Plug was, but there was something about this man's way of saying it, that made me swear inwardly that I would own a Genuine Mexican Plug, or die.

"Has he any other—er—advantages?" I inquired, suppressing what eagerness I could.   (Chapter XXIV)

Since this is both an initiation story and a tall tale, the narrator of course buys the horse, only to discover that his other advantages are that he can out-eat and "out-buck anything in America." Unable to rid himself of the horse any other way, he tells us, "I gave the Genuine Mexican Plug to a passing Arkansas emigrant whom fortune delivered into my hand. If this ever meets his eye, he will doubtless remember the donation."

Psychological tensions on the frontier exist not only between old-timers and newcomers, but also between the newcomer and his ideas about himself and his environment. Well beyond the Mexican Plug adventure, Mark Twain shows himself undergoing a more difficult kind of initiation. Here, as in the boot-black episode, the tall tale is not an instrument of initiation but a response to it. In Chapters 31 through 33, often reprinted as "Lost in the Snow," Mark Twain and his companions learn the irrelevance of literary solutions, traditional values, and conventional rhetoric in a world where survival depends upon clear thinking and practical action. Lost in a blizzard, abandoned by their horses, unable to light a fire, they make sentimental apologies for past injuries, renounce their bad habits, and give themselves up for dead, only to discover in the morning that they are still alive and have all along been fifteen steps from a stage station. When Mark Twain claims that he has "scarcely exaggerated a detail of this curious and absurd adventure" (p. 222), the conventional tall tale claim of truthfulness reminds us that he has exaggerated his adventures for the sake of a good story, but that the feelings expressed genuinely represent the feelings of that uncomfortable episode.

In portraying the psychological tensions evoked when old meets new on the frontier, Mark Twain presents himself as audience, victim, and creator of tall tales. Many of the tallest tales, especially in the early part of the book, are given to other narrators: Bemis, Johnson, Hyde, the stage driver. Mark Twain's growing skepticism and understanding of the genre appear like a refrain: "I made up my mind that if this man [Bemis] was not a liar he only missed it by the skin of his teeth," "This person's statements were not generally believed," and "some instinct or other made me set this Johnson down as being unreliable." Giving these very tall tales to other narrators allows Mark Twain to illustrate his own initiation, but more importantly it helps him to maintain his deadpan stance. He is harder to catch in a lie because his tales are more nearly possible that the stories of those other unreliable narrators.

Not the least of the inspirations for the tall tale in *Roughing It* is the magnificence of nature in the West. Most of the natural wonders described in the book had already been reported, either by eastern trav-·elers or by mountaineers and explorers like Jim Bridger, just as the treasures of Europe had been described to Americans before *The Innocents Abroad*. What Mark Twain adds to the knowledge of those who have stayed home is a demonstration of an attitude toward the West—an attitude conducive to the tall tale. Though the reader may already have heard of certain western wonders and peculiarities, some things are so marvelous, according to Mark Twain, that you cannot really know they are true unless you experience them yourself. The narrator of course knew of mountain peaks covered with "eternal snow," and yet when he finally saw white summits in August he "was full as much amazed as if he had never heard of snow in August before." "Truly, 'seeing is believing,'" he explains, "and many a man lives a long life through, *thinking* he believes certain universally received and well established things, and yet never suspects that if he were confronted by those things once, he would discover that he did not really believe them before, but only thought he believed them" (p. 107). The discovery of these levels of astonishment and belief prompts the narrator to further investigation and experimentation.

He finds the West full of wonders which inspire a creative mind to imagine even greater wonders. In Chapter 38, the description of the alkali lake, Mark Twain demonstrates the ease of slipping from the factual to the fantastic, using a technique often employed by folk narrators to confuse their victims or to draw their friends into a rollicking game of catch-me-if-you-can. Each paragraph begins with an apparently factual statement about the lake: "The lake is two hundred feet deep"; "a white man cannot drink the water of Mono Lake"; "Mono Lake is a hundred miles in a straight line from the ocean"; "there are only two seasons in the region round Mono Lake" (pp. 243–46). As each paragraph progresses, factual, believable statements lead to questionable statements and then to either pure fantasy or nonsense: a dog with many raw places on him fell into the lake, got out and ran in circles doing somersaults, and then "struck off over the mountains, at a gait which we estimated at about two hundred and fifty miles an hour, and he is going yet." He describes the wildlife found at Mono Lake, but then claims that "the ducks eat the flies—the flies eat the worms—the Indians eat all three—the wild cats eat the Indians—the white folks eat the wild cats—and thus all things are lovely." After each absurd ending, a new paragraph begins with a mild, factual statement, the cycle is repeated, and the reader again has no way of being sure at what point fact gives way to fantasy.

Finally, the narrator admits that some of his "facts" are less reliable than others.

So uncertain is the climate in Summer that a lady who goes out visiting cannot hope to be prepared for all emergencies unless she takes her fan under one arm and her snow shoes under the other. When they have a Fourth of July procession it generally snows on them, and they do say that as a general thing when a man calls for a brandy toddy there, the bar keeper chops it off with a hatchet and wraps it up in a paper, like maple sugar. And it is further reported that the old soakers haven't any teeth—wore them out eating gin cocktails and brandy punches. I do not endorse that statement—I simply give it for what it is worth—and it is worth—well, I should say, millions, to any man who can believe it without straining himself. But I do endorse the snow on the Fourth of July—because I know that to be true.   (p. 246)

Presumably he knows that to be true because he has seen it himself. Presumably. But where nature behaves in such extraordinary ways, wonder, as well as fear and pride, may be best expressed through the creation of extravagant fictions.

"The truth" in *Roughing It*, as James Cox explains in *The Fate of Humor*, "is not a series of facts, nor is it a transcendental reality hidden behind a world of dreams and shadows. It is rather the skeptical state of mind which the tall tale evokes in the listener, forcing him to maintain a questioning alertness in the face of experience."[5] But the truth in *Roughing It* is also the image of a wondrously tall world refracted by the mind of a humorist. And, finally, the truth in the tall tale of *Roughing It* is the revelation of the narrator's attitude toward his subject, his audience, and himself.

In a folk group, the narration of tall tales initiates novices, entertains the group, and delineates, binds, and celebrates the group. The narrator of *Roughing It*, by taking upon himself the role of tale teller, attempts to create the literary equivalent of a folk group among his readers and performs the functions of group raconteur.

From the beginning, Mark Twain offers the reader the opportunity to assume the role of an insider, of one who knows. The language of the first page ("and maybe get hanged or scalped, and have ever such a fine time") transparently reveals the appropriate bias: the reader must align himself with the old-timer if he wishes to avoid being ridiculous. The early discussion of "impossible reminiscences" told around a sagebrush campfire, followed by the story of the unwisely voracious camel, also clearly warns that much of the narrative will be woven from tall yarn. The reader who can enjoy the role of willing victim becomes a partner in creating the tales, discovers the tales' truths, and shares the narrator's peculiar perceptions and experiences.

Mark Twain encourages a feeling of intimacy by occasionally reminding the reader of his prior acquaintance with the author of *The Innocents Abroad*. The voracious camel story is only the first of several allusions to his travels in the Holy Land. In Chapter 6, he claims to quote from his Holy Land notebook a passage about the boy Jack's admiration for Overland Stage division agent Ben Holliday. Since no such entry appears in the extant Holy Land notebooks, the episode may have been invented especially for *Roughing It* as a deliberate attempt to establish a bond with the reader. At the same time, the episode suggests what kind of folk group the narrator would like to address and what group he repudiates. In response to the elderly pilgrim's enthusiastic oration about the wonder of Moses' guiding the children of Israel through the desert for forty years, Jack exclaims "*Forty years? Only three hundred miles?* Humph! Ben Holliday would have fetched them through in thirty-six hours!" (p. 74). To the eyes of the Vandal, the new world is at least as wonderful as the old. The stuffy pilgrim who appreciates only the greatness in books ranks with the tenderfoot who envied his brother's opportunity to get hanged or scalped. Together with the literary commonplaces and the Sunday School morality cast aside in "Lost in the Snow,"[6] they represent a culture outside the group that Mark Twain invites the reader to join.

As readers, our participation in the tall tale of *Roughing It* indoctrinates us into the ways of those who know and appreciate the American West. We can therefore flaunt our lack of cultivation, our ignorance

of or disregard for the cultural superiority of Europe, and our differences from excessively "gilded and filigreed" Americans.

The character assigned to the reader is not, however, identical to the
character of the narrator. In a folk group, the spinner of tall yarns often
borders on social deviance because of the openness of his disdain for
outsiders and because of his nonchalant approach to the distinction between fact and fiction. In *Roughing It*, the narrator's assumed character exaggerates the Vandal's traits and attitudes. He is more inclined
to stretch the truth, more outspoken and irreverent, more independent, more eccentric, and perhaps less cultivated than his readers
would really like to be; but because he is a self-created fool, the tale
of his errors and humiliations entertains the group without inviting
their contempt. In the end, his words conquer and control nature, fear,
failure, and outsiders, while his compelling revelation of the grandeur
of the West justifies and aggrandizes his own character.

The interplay of the tall West with his tall character reaches a climax
in the description of Mono Lake in Chapter 38. In the course of one
repetition of the cyclical pattern of fact and fantasy, the narrator reveals
himself:

Mono Lake is a hundred miles in a straight line from the ocean — and between it and the ocean are one or two ranges of mountains — yet thousands
of sea-gulls go there every season to lay their eggs and rear their young.
One would as soon expect to find sea-gulls in Kansas. And in this connection let us observe another instance of Nature's wisdom. The islands in the
lake being merely huge masses of lava, coated over with ashes and pumice
stone, and utterly innocent of vegetation or anything that would burn; and
the sea-gulls' eggs being entirely useless to anybody unless they be cooked,
Nature has provided an unfailing spring of boiling water on the largest
island, and you can put your eggs in there, and in four minutes you can
boil them as hard as any statement I have made during the past fifteen
years. (p. 245)

Cooking game in a boiling spring is a popular motif in folklore and
in folklore-inspired literature; boiling eggs "as hard as any statement
I have made during the past fifteen years" is a typical bit of Twainian
exhibitionism. He revels in his reputation as fact-stretcher; but he has
taught us, by this stage of the narrative, to be less concerned about fact
and fiction than about the pleasures of the tall tale experience.

After this climax at Mono Lake, the tall tale attitude and style begin
to disintegrate. The Blind Lead episode of Chapters 40 and 41 seems
to be fictionalized and makes an interesting story, but its tone is more
ironic than humorous and it lacks the timbre of the oral tale evident
in many earlier episodes. The closing claim of veracity has the form but
not the spirit of the tall tale coda:

It reads like a wild fancy sketch, but the evidence of many witnesses, and
likewise that of the official records of Esmeralda District, is easily obtain-
able in proof that it is a true history.   (p. 264)

This is very different from Bemis' "I wish I may rot in my tracks and
die the death of a dog if it isn't [true]" or the narrator's own "I am not
given to exaggeration, and when I say a thing I mean it" (p. 112). The
Blind Lead disclaimer is either an inappropriately overblown tall tale
ending or else an uncharacteristically serious attempt to emphasize fact
rather than fiction. In either case the disclaimer suggests that the narrator's character and attitude are shifting.[7]
    After Chapter 41, when the narrator has given up mining to become
a newspaperman, the tone of the book is increasingly literary and historical—less inspired by oral narrative and more openly concerned with
literary method and historical fact, less a creation of fiction and more
a recapitulation of newspaper reports. In Chapter 46, for example, he
takes the trouble to explain that in describing the Nevada nabobs he
has "shifted their occupations and experiences around in such a way
as to keep the Pacific public from recognizing" them (p. 293). In Chapter 50, he explains that although he is about to digress from his subject,
he will not apologize: "the information I am about to offer is apology
enough in itself. And since I digress constantly anyhow, perhaps it is
as well to eschew apologies altogether and thus prevent their growing
irksome" (p. 318). In Chapter 52 he escapes the need for such apology
by warning the reader that he wishes "to say an instructive word or two
about the silver mines, [and] the reader may take this fair warning and
skip, if he chooses" (p. 337). Finally, in Chapter 60, he does offer an
apology: "I have dwelt at some length upon this matter of pocket mining because it is a subject that is seldom referred to in print, and therefore I judged that it would have for the reader that interest which naturally attaches to novelty" (p. 389). Instead of playfully blurring the
boundary between fact and fiction, he carefully documents his reports;

and instead of attempting to simulate the oral style's direct contact between narrator and reader, he continually reminds us that the printed book intervenes. We are no longer fellow travelers invited to join him at his campfire and learn about his world through wonderful tales; instead we are readers invited to sit at home by our own fires and read a book which may occasionally tire us with dry instruction.

There is humor in this section, but it too retreats from the tall tale style. Gone is the deadpan narrator innocently (but slyly) uttering absurdities, exaggerating his own misadventures, and illuminating his own eccentric character. The new narrator, more openly humorous, tells comic stories and portrays comic types. The Nevada nabobs in New York City, in typical country-lout-in-the-city fashion, attempt to hire an omnibus for their private carriage. "Buck Fanshaw's Funeral" portrays a rather conventional misunderstanding between a gentlemanly newcomer and a local rough, where the narrator identifies with neither character. The narrator does exaggerate the comic contrasts of the frontier, but he does so as an outsider who observed or heard of comic occurences, rather than as an insider who feels the pressures of these contrasts and creates fiction in response to those pressures.

This detachment from humorous incident increases in Chapter 55, which contains three rather tired anecdotes about drunkards, and Chapter 56, which reports, but does not really tell, a tall tale. Rather than telling the story in the form of a reminiscence elaborated with authenticating detail, as he does in his best imitations of skillful oral style, the narrator generalizes, summarizes, and italicizes the tale. He tells of "a very, very wicked soldier" who died at Fort Yuma, "went straight to the hottest corner of perdition,—and the next day he *telegraphed back for his blankets*" (p. 368). Years later, Mark Twain would complain that the European tendency to italicize the nub of a comic story "is very depressing, and makes one want to renounce joking and lead a better life."[8]

Even in the most skillfully written humor of this section the narrator maintains his literary stance. The story of Jim Blaine and his Grandfather's Old Ram is a frame tale in which the narrator discovers at the end that he has been "sold." While the story may be seen as an initiation hoax, it emphasizes not the frame narrator's awakening but Jim Blaine's comic maundering. In Chapter 61, Mark Twain again assumes the role of frame narrator when he reports the story of Dick Baker and his prospecting cat, Tom Quartz. It is a tall tale, told with great serious-

ness "whenever [Jim] was out of luck and a little down hearted," about
the cat's extraordinary sagacity and remarkable survival of a blasting
mishap. While the tale reflects the gentle miner's own preference for
pocket mining over quartz blasting, it reveals little about the frame narrator, who plays a sympathetic but peripheral role in its telling:

> I said, "Well, Mr. Baker, his prejudice against quartz mining *was* re-
> markable, considering how he came by it. Couldn't you ever cure him of
> it?"
> "Cure him! No! When Tom Quartz was sot once, he was *always* sot—
> and you might a blowed him up as much as three million times 'n' you'd
> never a broken him of his cussed prejudice agin quartz mining."
> The affection and the pride that lit up Baker's face when he delivered
> this tribute to the firmness of his humble friend of other days, will always
> be a vivid memory with me.   (p. 393)

The frame narrator Mark Twain participates in the telling of this tale
much as George does in the Sut Lovingood *Yarns*. He has become a
literary man who observed and occasionally participated in the frontier
life he reports, rather than a character who defines and creates himself
through the humorous exaggeration of his own experiences.

For this new narrator, the tall tale has lost both the immediacy and
the usefulness that it had in the earlier part of the book. At the end
of Chapter 58, where he reports a missed opportunity to travel to New
York and make his fortune selling a silver mine, he laments his loss:
"Let us not dwell on this miserable matter. If I were inventing these
things, I could be wonderfully humorous over them; but they are too
true to be talked of with hearty levity, even at this distant day" (p. 379).
He later learned, he adds in a footnote, that the man who went to New
York in his stead actually received far less than the million dollars originally reported in the newspapers. And so this episode adheres no more
closely to the facts than many an earlier misadventure which he dwelt
on at length and "talked of with hearty levity." Even if it were entirely
factual, the tall tale's great utility is that it can alleviate discomfort by
transforming "miserable matter" into wonderful humor. But by this
point in the narrative Mark Twain has for the most part ceased to be
a spinner of tall yarns.

In Chapters 62 through 77, Mark Twain leaves the American West
and heads for the Sandwich Islands. Reworking material from letters
written to the *Sacramento Union* in 1866, he abandons the letters'

simplistic contrast between the gentlemanly Mr. Twain and the boorish Mr. Brown, and attempts to create an intermediate single voice that can deliver fact, sentiment, and humor simultaneously, or a least sequentially. This new voice occasionally sounds like the poker-faced humorist of the earlier part of *Roughing It*. Transcribing almost verbatim from an uncharacteristic portion of a *Union* letter, he describes his excursion on the horse Oahu: "I said, never mind—I preferred a safe horse to a fast one—a horse with no spirit whatever—a lame one, if he had such a thing" (p. 409). Other bits of humor in this section, however, depend upon a rather heavy-handed irony:

[human sacrifices atoned for sins] long before the missionaries braved a thousand privations to come and make them permanently miserable by telling them how beautiful and how blissful a place heaven is, and how nearly impossible it is to get there; and showed the poor native how dreary a place perdition is and what unnecessarily liberal facilities there are for going to it; showed him how, in his ignorance, he had gone and fooled away all his kinfolks to no purpose; showed him what rapture it is to work all day long for fifty cents to buy food for the next day with, as compared with fishing for pastime and lolling in the shade through eternal summer, and eating the bounty that nobody labored to provide but Nature. How sad it is to think of the multitudes who have gone to their graves in this beautiful island and never knew there was a hell! (pp. 411–412)

Although the gentleman and the boor are gone and the new narrator speaks in a more appealing voice, he rarely attempts congenial humor. Subject and tone both reveal that the material was tossed in largely to reach the subscription book's expected length. His original purpose, too, was different. In his letters from Hawaii, Mark Twain had been reporting for a newspaper on a land and culture which most of his readers would never see, which would have little real influence on their personalities and their lives, and which had not shaped his own character.

In *Roughing It*, he is not simply reporting a new world, but discovering it, partly inventing it, and showing how it inspired his extravagant humor and his exuberant independence. The frontier had always been, and the Far West was now becoming, an essential component in the world's image of America and Americanness. In the first forty-one chapters of *Roughing It*, Mark Twain solidifies and celebrates this image of the American by telling the tall tale of the American West, and by creating a peculiarly American character—Mark Twain, teller of tales.

CHAPTER 6

Mark Twain:
Remembering Anything, Whether it Happened or Not

That book was made by Mr. Mark Twain and he told the truth, mainly.

—Huck Finn

Twenty-five years after the publication of *Roughing It* Mark Twain began in earnest his final literary tall tale: his autobiography. In *Roughing It*, the tall tale of the American West revealed cultural, more than personal, truths. The *Autobiography* tells the tall tale of Mark Twain.

From the beginning, Mark Twain impresses upon us that this is not an ordinary autobiography. In the preface he explains that, because the work is not to be published until after his death, he is "speaking from the grave" and can therefore speak his "whole frank mind." Comparing an autobiography to a love letter exposed in a breach-of-promise suit and published in the papers, he explains that the erstwhile lover "cannot find anything in the letter that was not true, honest and respectworthy; but no matter, he would have been very much more reserved if he had known he was writing for print."[1] In preparing a posthumous autobiography, Mark Twain reasons, he can be "as frank and free and unembarrassed as a love letter." He leaves us to discover to what extent and in what manner the work will be true.

The matter of truth arises again in Albert Bigelow Paine's preface to the first edition, where the editor and literary executor felt compelled to offer readers a warning and an explanation, much as a folk yarnspinner's friends may offer superfluous apologies and assurances to a visiting folklorist. Paine assures readers that, although the actual facts of Mark Twain's life have sometimes been embellished or misstated, "Mark Twain's soul was built of the very fabric of truth, so far as moral intent was concerned" (Paine, I, xi). Paine's explanation of Mark Twain's deviations from fact is just: the author's memory sometimes failed him in matters of dates and small details, his imagination was often prompted by prejudice, and habit often led him to turn fact into a "good story" (Paine, I, xi). Paine's apology indicates that this is not an ordinary biography in which the facts of the author's life are illuminated and interpreted through his personal perspective and understanding, but an autobiography in which "facts" are created to illustrate moral, emotional, psychological, and cultural truths. It is in many respects a fiction cast in the form of autobiography, creating a tall character, expanding and enlarging fact to comic improbability, managing stress through comic intervention, teasing and challenging readers—in many respects a tall tale.

Mark Twain, too, warns readers of his factual inaccuracies. His warnings, however, are not self-conscious apologies, like Paine's, but self-congratulatory celebrations of his comic invention: "When I was younger I could remember anything, whether it happened or not; but my faculties are decaying now, and soon I shall be so I cannot remember any but the things that never happened. It is sad to go to pieces like this, but we all have to do it" (Paine, I, 96). He repeatedly reminds us of his tendency to elaborate: his "facts" have always had a "substratum of truth" (Paine, I, 293); his mother very early learned the art of extracting that truth by discounting him "90 per cent for embroidery" (Paine, I, 294); Joe Twichell came over from Hartford "to take dinner and stay all night and swap some lies" (Paine, I, 334); and, after the story of selling a dog to General Miles, "Now then, that is the tale. Some of it is true" (DeVoto, 358).

To combine autobiography and fiction was not new to Mark Twain. He had done it in *The Innocents Abroad, Roughing It, Old Times on the Mississippi,* even *Tom Sawyer* and *Huckleberry Finn.* Even explicitly to call it autobiography was not new. That he had done whenever he told a tall tale; folk narrators do it without a blush or a hint. Reporting on tale tellers in the Okefenokee Swamp Rim, Kay Cothran explored the relationship between historical autobiography and tall tale autobiography:

The excellent storyteller, who does to a degree depend on his storytelling for the esteem of those not belonging to his Society, must to that degree live the "lie" and bring his social self into line with his persona in tall tales. . . . The storyteller develops his image as an eccentric. Lies (tall tales) become truth. Asked for his biography, Lem Griffis interwove fact and fantasy. . . . Yet if asked pointedly, Lem could shift gears entirely and give information which he believed absolutely factual.[2]

In his *Autobiography* Mark Twain shifts back and forth frequently, smoothly, and often imperceptibly.

This shifting back and forth between fact and fiction is facilitated by the form of the *Autobiography*, which is desultory, undisciplined, fickle. Some of it Mark Twain wrote out by hand; most of it he dictated. Some sections are long narratives, others short anecdotes or comments. Frequently he read into it a letter or an extract from the day's newspaper, and then dictated whatever reactions, interpretations, or reminiscences the piece inspired. The arrangement of the disparate sections was to be, not chronological, but the haphazard order of their creation. This fluidity of form allows Mark Twain to tie his tall tales into past fact or present moment—just as the folk yarnspinner introduces tall tales into casual conversation, leading his listeners, unwarned and unaware, into a fantasy world. Because much of the *Autobiography is* historically accurate, the autobiographical framework provides a structural and rhetorical deadpan for tall tale fiction.

The method is also limiting. In a letter to William Dean Howells, Mark Twain complained of several disadvantages he found in dictating an autobiography, among them a fear of offending the religious principles or feminine delicacy of his stenographers.[3] There is almost no sex or scatology in the book, and there is no complete picture of his theology. Significantly, two of the most personal, emotional passages in the *Autobiography* — accounts of the deaths of Livy and Jean—were not dictated but written out by hand. A natural human reticence about one's own flaws also hindered him:

I have been dictating this autobiography of mine daily for three months. I have thought of fifteen hundred or two thousand incidents in my life which I am ashamed of but I have not gotten one of them to consent to go on paper yet. I think that that stock will still be complete and unimpaired when I finish this autobiography, if I ever finish it. I believe that if I should put in all those incidents I would be sure to strike them out when I came to revise this book.   (Neider, 224)

Even the anxiety-releasing tall tale is not competent to exorcise the most serious flaws, the very deepest bereavements, and the bitterest philosophies. Where such feelings are approached in the *Autobiography*, they appear in ironic or sarcastic homilies ("I believe our heavenly father invented man because he was disappointed in the monkey," De-Voto, 372) or in intensely personal laments ("Jean lies there, and I sit here—writing, busying myself, to keep my heart from breaking," Neider, 372). Through most of the work, however, the darkest side of Mark Twain's soul is set aside; self-revelation is light-hearted or indirect.[4]

If the *Autobiography* was not intended to be a confessional or to reveal all the facts, mistakes, and disappointments of Mark Twain's life, it was nevertheless intended to reveal his character. "Certainly," he tells us, "a biography's chiefest feature is the exhibition of the *character* of the man whose biography is being set forth" (Paine, I, 288). A conventional biography would be inadequate for Mark Twain and a full biography can never be written because life consists mainly not of "facts and happenings" but of "the storm of thoughts that is forever blowing through one's head" (Paine, I, 288).

The character Mark Twain chose most to reveal was his public character, Mark Twain the writer, lecturer, yarnspinner; and like a folk raconteur shaping his biography to suit his public image and his character to suit his imaginary biography, Mark Twain deliberately developed a tall character living a tall life. He assumed the character of the eiron—the braggart who makes himself out to be worse than he actually is—as opposed to the alazon, who boasts a glory he does not deserve.[5] The character had been suggested and developed in many earlier works. In *The Innocents Abroad* he flaunted and exaggerated his lack of cultivation; in his *(Burlesque) Autobiography*, published in 1871, he claimed to be descended from thieves; in *Roughing It* he described himself as lazy and irresponsible; in "The Private History of a Campaign that Failed" he confessed to being a disorderly, reluctant soldier and ultimately a deserter; in *A Tramp Abroad* he used his own laziness as a comic contrast to the frivolous heroics of alpinistes.

The *Autobiography* re-creates both the inclination to sloth and the penchant for social blundering. Comparing himself to Henry Rogers

In 1906, Albert Bigelow Paine took this series of photographs of Mark Twain in Dublin, New Hampshire. Mark Twain sent sets to several of his friends and specified that the pictures should be placed in his *Autobiography*. The inscriptions and his caption clearly show his delight in the role of moral backslider:

This series of photographs registers with scientific precision, stage by stage, the progress of a moral purpose through the mind of the human race's Oldest Friend.

From Charles Neider's edition of the *Autobiography*. Photographs courtesy of the Mark Twain Project, the Bancroft Library.

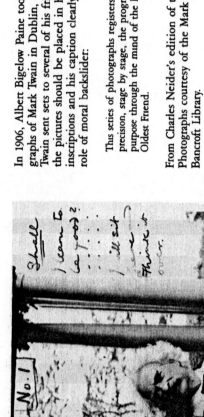

No. 5

... But there I couldn't invest the Scale ...

No. 4

... and just put my whole heart into it ...

of the Standard Oil Company, he claims "I was born to indolence, idleness, procrastination, indifference—the qualities that constitute a shirk" (Paine, I, 264). More joyous are his confessions of defective manners, especially the incurable cursing and smoking, and the social errors which inspired the ritual of "dusting off papa" after a dinner engagement. Occasionally the undersocialized tale teller claims a wiliness that suggests his social clumsiness may be cultivated, elaborated, even invented. Describing his halting, difficult, but ultimately successful courtship of the sheltered young heiress Olivia Langdon, he tells how he fell from his departing carriage and in an inspired moment feigned unconsciousness, thereby gaining an extension of his visit. In an earlier account of this incident, written in a letter to Mary Fairbanks a week after the accident occurred, he claims that he broke his neck "in eleven different places and lay there about four or five minutes, completely insensible."[6] The differently embellished version in the *Autobiography*, with its Tom Sawyerish trick, better suits his character as a social misfit married to a lady.

That exaggerated character is both artist and work of art. Like moving his uncle John Quarles' farm from Missouri to Arkansas for *Huckleberry Finn*, the elaborations of his character are justifiable as art. He moved the farm "all of six hundred miles but it was no trouble; it was not a very large farm—five hundred acres, perhaps—but I could have done it if it had been twice as large. And as for the morality of it, I cared nothing for that; I would move a state if the exigencies of literature required it" (Neider, 4). Lies and exaggerations, too, can be works of art and may be justified. Fulminating over Thomas Rees's claim that the Snodgrass letters were written under contract and paid for at the time of publication, Mark Twain incidentally explains which falsehoods are justified and which are not:

Those two statements are plain straightforward falsehoods; and what is more, and worse, they are poorly devised, unplausible, and inartistic. As works of art, even a Rees ought to be ashamed of them I think.   (DeVoto, 239)

To Mark Twain, a well-crafted fiction carries some kind of truth, and the artist is both professional liar and professional truth-teller. After repeatedly accusing President Roosevelt of lying, exaggerating, and "showing off," he asks "Hasn't he tacitly claimed some dozens of times that he is the only person in America who knows how to speak the truth—quite ignoring me and other professionals?" (DeVoto, 20). Like folk narrators who playfully blur the distinctions between truth, lies, and fiction, he is deliberately ambiguous. In a straight reading of the sentence Mark Twain is an artist who reveals truth; in a comic reading he is as unregenerate a liar as Roosevelt. In the conjunction of the two meanings, we find the character of the tall tale artist.

Portraits of other people in the *Autobiography* are filtered through or reflected off this yarnspinning character. "This autobiography of mine is a mirror," he explains, "and I am looking at myself in it all the time. Incidentally I notice the people that pass along at my back" (Paine, II, 312). As he notices those people and events that appear in his mirror, he describes not their historical, factual existence but their reflection on the mirror of his mind. Writing about his mother, he proposes not to give her formal history, but to take illustrative extracts from it, to "furnish flashlight glimpses of her character, not a professional view of her career. Technically speaking, she had no career; but she had a character, and it was of a fine and striking and lovable sort" (Paine, I, 115). He tells the story of her sympathetic defense of Satan—a defense beguiled out of her by conspirators who claimed she would say a soft word for the devil himself. "Who prays for Satan?" she demanded. None of us is saved through his own effort and merit alone; but "who, in eighteen centuries, has had the common humanity to pray for the one sinner that needed it most?" (Neider, 26). That story may be true. Historically accurate or not, it is true to Mark Twain's conception of his mother's "fine and striking and lovable" character; it accurately reveals the reflection of her character upon his.

In the discussion of Bret Harte, all of Harte's actions are colored by Mark Twain's reactions. He uses the *Autobiography* to express and perhaps exorcise his anger and indignation. Generously but briefly praising Harte's talent, he says that even when Harte worked rapidly his "work was good and usable; to me it was a wonderful performance. . . . His part [of the collaboration *Ah Sin*] was the best part of it" (DeVoto, 277–78). Mark Twain dwells, however, on Harte's arrogance, irresponsibility, and insensitivity. His statements go well beyond a description of the man's character: Harte "hadn't a sincere fibre in him. I think he was incapable of emotion, for I think he had nothing to feel with. I think his heart was merely a pump and had no other function" (DeVoto, 265); "I think the sense of shame was left out of Harte's constitution" (p. 281); "He hadn't any more passion for his country than an oyster has for its bed; in fact not so much and I apologize to the oyster. The higher passions were left out of Harte; what he knew about them he got from books" (p. 286). In reaction to Howells' claim that Harte was one of the wittiest persons he had ever met, Mark Twain offers his own opinion of the nature of Harte's wit: "It possessed no breadth and no variety; it consisted solely of sneers and sarcasms; when there was nothing to sneer at, Harte did not flash and sparkle and was not more entertaining than the rest of us" (pp. 274-75). The metaphors, anec-dotes, and diatribes may not present a well-rounded view of Harte's life and character; but they clearly reveal a part of Mark Twain's char-acter by exhibiting his offended pride, outraged morality, and a touch of jealousy. The tenor of the work as a whole—its tallness and its avowed purpose to reveal the self rather than the facts—encourages us to un-derstand, excuse, and even respect Mark Twain's exaggeration of Bret Harte's faults. Like Sut Lovingood controlling chaos through comic artis-try or Don Lewis conquering fear through laughter, Mark Twain tri-umphs over his artistic, moral, or commercial adversaries by reliving his conflicts with them in an exaggerated, even created, tall world.

Other tales are told more purely for the pleasure of the telling. The joy of beginning with a preposterous premise, following it to its logical conclusions, and accumulating comic details along the way motivates stories like the marvelous tale about Joe Twichell's green hair. One Sat-urday night Twichell, the Congregationalist minister in Hartford and one of Mark Twain's closest friends, found a bottle of what he thought was hair restorer; he "gave his head a good drenching and sousing with it . . . and thought no more about it. Next morning when he got up his head was bright green!" The logic of the tale requires that Twichell should be unable to find a substitute preacher and should have only the most grave of sermons to preach. "The gravity of the sermon did not harmonize with the gayety of his head, and the people sat all through it with their handkerchiefs stuffed in their mouths—any way to try to keep down their joy. And Twichell told me that he never had seen his [entire congregation] absorbed in interest in his sermon, from beginning to end, before." Human nature dictates that the people not only should be absorbed in the sermon but should also wait "to shake him by the hand and tell him what a good sermon it was," though "it was quite plain they were not interested in the sermon at all; they only wanted to get a near view of his head."

At this point Mark Twain more directly reveals his own involvement in the story and his pleasure in telling it: "Well, Twichell said—no, Twichell didn't say, *I* say, that as the days went on and Sunday followed Sunday, the interest in Twichell's hair grew and grew; because it didn't stay green. It took on deeper and deeper shades of green; and then it would become reddish, and it would go from that to some other color . . . and Twichell's head became famous." The story ends with a typical tall tale statement of the significance of these events, with the humorous intent leaking out only in the ironic use of the word "business": "And it was good thing in several ways, because the business had been languishing a little, and now a lot of people joined the church so that they could have the show, and it was the beginning of a prosperity for that church which has never diminished in all these years. Nothing so fortunate ever happened to Joe as that" (Paine, I, 342–44).

Thus speaks the tale teller as performer. Occasionally, however, he claims only to be performing for himself, to enjoy talking along without the bother of being sensitive to an audience. For his own satisfaction he takes for his text whatever is uppermost in his mind:

I don't seem to get done with any text—but it doesn't matter, I am not interested in getting done with anything. I am only interested in talking along and wandering around as much as I want to, regardless of results for the future reader. (Paine, I, 327)

This apparent disregard for the reader, although partly a genuine expression of the pleasures of unrestrained talk, is also partly a pose. He repeatedly expresses his interest in the reactions of his future readers, justifying his combination of diary and history not only by the pleasure the form brings him, but by the fascination that "news," written in the language and with the fresh interest of the present, will have for readers a hundred years in the future (Paine, I, 322–27). His own interest in the reactions of those distant readers is clearly indicated in another letter to Howells:

To-morrow I mean to dictate a chapter which will get my heirs & assigns burnt alive if they venture to print it this side of 2006 A.D.—which I judge they won't. There'll be lots of such chapters if I live 3 or 4 years longer. The edition of A.D. 2006 will make a stir when it comes out. I shall be hovering around taking notice, along with other dead pals. You are invited.[7]

Although, as Paine points out, Mark Twain's philosophical views were
not particularly new or shocking even in 1905 when *What Is Man?* was
privately printed,[8] he clearly enjoyed the prospect of posthumously continuing in the role of social misfit and philosophical iconoclast. Finally
his enjoyment of the work led him to abandon the idea of speaking
only from the grave, and he published portions of the *Autobiography*
in the *North American Review* between September 1906 and December 1907.

The teller of tall tales exhibits his tall character, exorcises his fears
and angers, and enjoys the role of performer; but he also spins his yarns
in the context of a group, creating a bond among those who recognize,
understand, and enjoy the tale. By assuming that readers of this *Autobiography* will appreciate his tall tales, Mark Twain casts the reader in
the role of friend, insider, privileged listener. Howells wrote, in 1901,
that Mark Twain's "personal books" (*Innocents, Roughing It, Life on
the Mississippi, A Tramp Abroad, Following the Equator*) overshadow
his fiction, for "they are an immediate and most informal hospitality
which admits you at once to the author's confidence, and makes you
frankly welcome not only to his thought but to his way of thinking."[9]
The *Autobiography* carries this technique and this characteristic attitude to its furthest extreme.

He now delights in speaking to a far larger group than he had imagined himself to be addressing in *Roughing It*. He is read and has lec-
tured around the world, and he cannot resist a veiled boast. Complaining about the rigidities and inadequacies of the American postal system,
he quotes some of the odd addresses on letters sent him:

>Mark Twain
>   Somewhere

>Mark Twain
>   God Knows Where

and finally

>Mark Twain
>   Somewhere
>   (Try Satan)

That stranger's trust was not misplaced. Satan courteously sent it along.
(Paine, II, 241–24)

Again the eiron speaks, making himself out to be of special interest to Satan, but at the same time innocently reveling in the flattery of being found by a letter so vaguely directed. The post office, even without an address, can always find him. He would like to be yarnspinner and social misfit for the world.

In deliberately and openly inviting into his confidence so large and diverse a group as readers around the world and down the centuries, Mark Twain expands the functions of the oral tall tale, as so large a work must do. Nonetheless he does try to create that intimacy, and he does so largely through the tallness of the work. To appreciate the tales, the reader must know the author's life and his work, and must have an almost personal interest in the workings of his mind, in the "storm of thoughts" blowing through his head. To this reader Mark Twain confidently addresses himself, spinning his tall yarns with little concern for either his own credibility or the reader's gullibility. His character as tall tale artist was well established in his books and in the popular mind. The implied reader—an insider, an old acquaintance—must approach the work asking not "how much of this can we confidently add to Samuel Clemens' biography?" but, as with all tall fiction, "what is the nature of this character, Mark Twain? What is he trying to tell us about his world?" and, more importantly, "what fun can be had from submitting to or joining in this tall tale?"

CHAPTER 7

The Way the Natives Talk:
A Note on Colloquial Style

His manner was so singular, that half of his story consisted in his
excellent way of telling it.

—"The Big Bear of Arkansas"

The literature that brought tall humor into print, that created tall tale
relationships between authors and narrators and readers, and that sometimes created a sense of community through collective appreciation
of tall tales also helped to bring about significant changes in American
prose style, for as the tall tale moved from the tributaries and back-
waters of literature into the mainstream, it carried along with it the colloquial style.

The patterns of speech which we hear in the tales of oral yarnspinners were first adaped to print by writers quoting or mimicking actual
tale tellers. In Don Lewis' tale about a nighttime encounter with a bear-
sized rat, the repetition of simple constructions creates a rhythmic climax at the narrative climax of the tale:

The legs went underneath, the cot came down, I rolled out, it was pitch
black and—absolutely scared me to death. It was like wrestlin' with an
alligator: you had to stay out of the way of the tail.

The same syntactic and rhythmic patterns appear at the climax of a
well-known passage from *Sketches and Eccentricities of Colonel David*

Crockett (1833), where Davy tries unsuccessfully to grin a raccoon out of a tree.

I went over to the house, got my axe, returned to the tree, saw the 'coon was still there, and began to cut away. Down it come, and I run forward; but damn the 'coon was there to be seen.[1]

The 'coon, Davy discovers, was actually a knot in the tree.

The yarnspinning cowboy Van Holyoak used short, repetitive rhythmic patterns not just to create a climax but also to reinforce his poker face and create humor, by stating the possible and the absurd in rhythmically equivalent phrases:

[One day Grandfather attempted to jump the Grand Canyon.] He run right up to the edge of it and made 'im a merry hell of a jump, 'n he lacked about twenty feet of gettin' to the far side of it, and seen he wasn't gonna make it so he turned around and went back.

Mark Twain's Simon Wheeler uses the same technique to create, in print, the poker-faced stance, as well as to emphasize a crucial aspect of Jim Smiley's character:

He was the curiousest man about always betting on anything that turned up you ever see . . . if there was a dog-fight, he'd bet on it; if there was a cat-fight, he'd bet on it; if there was a chicken-fight, he'd bet on it; why if there was two birds setting on a fence, he would bet you which one would fly first; or if there was a camp-meeting, he would be there reg'lar to bet on Parson Walker, which he judged to be the best exhorter about here, and so he was too, and a good man.[2]

That Mark Twain intends to contrast Simon's speech with formal, written prose is evident from the structural complexity of the frame narrator's opening sentence:

In compliance with the request of a friend of mine, who wrote me from the East, I called on good-natured, garrulous old Simon Wheeler, and inquired after my friend's friend, Leonidas W. Smiley, as requested to do, and I hereunto append the result.[3]

Repetition of short, simple constructions cannot alone re-create in print the textures of oral style—the varying rhythms, the changes in pitch, the pauses, turns, and asides. A sample of the variety of tricks for echoing oral style can be found in the dialect portions of Mark Twain's *Roughing It*. The story of Dick Baker's cat Tom Quartz is presented as a frame tale, but the frame narrator has little need to describe to us Dick's style. The oral narrator's solemn demeanor is suggested by Baker's insistence on the cat's dignity ("he wouldn't let the Gov'ner of Californy be familar with him. He never ketched a rat in his life—'peared to be above it") and by his asides which tie the story to everyday life ("But that cat, you know, was *always* agin new fangled arrangements—somehow he never could abide 'em. *You* know how it is with old habits"). To suggest the rhythmic variations of a skillful oral narrator, Mark Twain slows the reader with long vowel sounds and a long clause, and then quickens the pace with sharp sounds and short phrases: "He didn't want no better prospect 'n that—'n' then he would lay down on our coats and snore like a steamboat till we'd struck a pocket, an' than get up 'n' superintend. He was nearly lightnin' on superintending."[4]

The carefully placed pause, so important to Mark Twain's platform lecturing technique and described in "How to Tell a Story," is created in print with dashes, innocuous filler phrases, and abrupt rhythmic changes. The climax of Dick Baker's tale requires four pauses. The first is suggested by a rhythmic change: several short phrases strung together with conjunctions lead suddenly to a longer phrase and a period.

Well, one day when the shaft was down about eight foot, the rock got so hard that we had to put in a blast—the first blast'n' we'd ever done since Tom Quartz was born. An' then we lit the fuse 'n' forgot 'n' left Tom Quartz sound asleep on the gunny sack.

The reader, compelled by the rhythmic change to pause here, needs only an instant to imagine the coming explosion. The second narrative pause is created by the filler "you know" and a repetition of Baker's resigned "it warn't no use."

In 'bout a minute we seen a puff of smoke bust up out of the hole, 'n' then everything let go with an awful crash, 'n' about four million ton of rocks 'n' dirt 'n' smoke 'n' splinters shot up 'bout a mile an' a half into the air, an' by George, right in the dead centre of it was old Tom Quartz a-goin' end over end, an' a-snortin' an' a-sneezin, an' a-clawin' an' a-reachin' for things like all possessed. But it warn't no use, you know, it warn't no use.

Narrative movement must stop here while the reader's imagination predicts the complete annihilation of Tom Quartz. That expectation is then, of course, overturned.

An' that was the last we see of *him* [another brief pause here] for about two minutes 'n' a half, an' then all of a sudden it begin to rain rocks and rubbage, an' directly he come down ker-whop, about ten foot off f'm where we stood. Well, I reckon he was p'raps the orneriest lookin' beast you ever see. One ear was sot back on his neck, 'n' his tail was stove up, 'n' his eye-winkers was swinged off, 'n' he was all blacked up with powder an' smoke, an' all sloppy with mud 'n' slush f'm one end to the other. Well sir, it warn't no use to try to apologize — we couldn't say a word.

The dash and the repetitive filler "we couldn't say a word" bring the reader to another brief halt, long enough to wonder what this marvelous cat will do next.

He took a sort of a disgusted look at hisself, 'n' then he looked at us — an' it was just exactly the same as if he had said — "Gents, maybe *you* think it's smart to take advantage of a cat that 'ain't had no experience of quartz minin', but *I* think different" — an' then he turned on his heel 'n' marched off home without ever saying another word. (392)

The Mark Twain narrator in *Roughing It*, though he generally does not speak in dialect, also uses a colloquial prose style. Richard Bridgman has defined colloquial style as "any prose written as if it were spoken" and has identified three primary characteristics of the American colloquial style: stress on the individual verbal unit, a resulting fragmentation of syntax, and the use of repetition to bind and unify.[5] Even in the second half of *Roughing It*, where he has shifted to a more literary attitude, Mark Twain's style is still colloquial. The driving rhythms of his prose appear in the book both early and late. In Chapter 5 he writes

The cayote is a living, breathing allegory of Want. He is *always* hungry. He is always poor, out of luck and friendless. The meanest creatures despise him and even the fleas would desert him for a velocipede. He is so spiritless and cowardly that even while his exposed teeth are pretending a threat, the rest of his face is apologizing for it. And he is *so* homely! — so scrawny, and ribby, and coarse-haired, and pitiful. (67)

and in Chapter 57

It was a driving, vigorous, restless population in those days. It was a *curi-ous* population. It was the *only* population of the kind that the world has ever seen gathered together, and it is not likely that the world will ever see its like again. . . . No women, no children, no gray and stooping veter-ans,—none but erect, bright-eyed, quick moving, strong-handed young giants—the strangest population, the finest population, the most gallant host that ever trooped down the startled solitudes of an unpeopled land. (370)

The changes and uncertainty of Mark Twain's narrative stance do, how-ever, lead him into inconsistencies of style, and the book contains many passages in which complex ideas are expressed not through repetition and expansion but through dense, complex sentence constructions. Chapter 55 ends with such a passage:

But for the journalistic monopoly that forbade the slightest revealment of Eastern news till a day after its publication in the California papers, the glorified flag on Mount Davidson [strangely lit up by the setting sun] would have been saluted and re-saluted, that memorable evening, as long as there was a charge of powder to thunder with; the city would have been illuminated, and every man that had any respect for himself would have got drunk,—as was the custom of the country on all occasions of public moment. Even at this distant day I cannot think of this needlessly marred supreme opportunity without regret. What a time we might have had!

Perhaps this is a deliberate use of mixed style. The news of the Union victory at Gettysburg brings out in the narrator his connection with the eastern states, which Mark Twain still associated with formal prose. Here the conventional patriot for the moment overrules the frontier in-dividualist and iconoclast, and his style reflects the shift. The change is short-lived, however, for the vernacular speaker reenters in the last sentence. Having once discovered him Mark Twain cannot abandon him for long.

In his later works, whether writing in his own voice or speaking through a first person narrator, Mark Twain continued to develop and perfect the colloquial style:

Once a day a cheap, gaudy packet arrived upward from St. Louis, and another downward from Keokuk. Before these events, the day was glorious with expectancy; after them, the day was a dead and empty thing. Not only the boys, but the whole village felt this.

"Old Times on the Mississippi," 1875

I am an American. I was born and reared in Hartford, in the State of Connecticut—anyway just over the river, in the country. So I am a Yankee of the Yankees—and practical; yes, and nearly barren of sentiment, I suppose—or poetry, in other words.

A Connecticut Yankee in King Arthur's Court, 1889

It was many years ago. Hadleyburg was the most honest and upright town in all the region round about it. It had kept that reputation unsmirched during three generations, and was prouder of it than of any other of its possessions.   "The Man That Corrupted Hadleyburg," 1899

The language is not dialect, nor is it primitive in any way. But its structures are loose and expansive, rather than complex and densely interwoven; its resonances are colloquial, oral.

In the early days of American humor, dialect narrators were employed for humor and local color. "The way the natives sometimes talk here is amusing," wrote the author of "'Old Sense,' of Arkansas"; and in many a frame tale the dialect speaker's voice contrasts humorously with the controlling, civilized voice of the frame narrator. But as writers like Thorpe, Harris and Mark Twain discovered the usefulness of the dialect character's viewpoint, dialect passages became ever longer: the civilizing voice of frame narrator or implied author yielded to the oral style of vernacular speakers. Jim Doggett, in Thorpe's "The Big Bear of Arkansas," speaks in a voice far more compelling, with language far more vivid than does the frame narrator who introduces him. Sut Lovingood's wild and difficult language reflects not just Harris' amusement with dialect but Sut's own raucous, irreverent view of the world. In *Roughing It,* Mark Twain developed a vernacular-speaking persona to represent the yarnspinning American and the American West. By the time Mark Twain finished with the tall tale, framing narrators and authorial voices had disappeared, and his own voice had completely adopted a colloquial style. In the twentieth century, even writers who make no use of tall tale exaggeration or yarnspinners have been influenced by the tall tale, for they use a colloquial style which found its way into American literature in the work of writers intent on mimicking the spoken style of oral yarnspinners.

Epilogue

"Truth is our most valuable commodity. Therefore let us economize it."
— Hal Holbrook in *Mark Twain Tonight*

Winter in upstate New York is known for its low temperatures, heavy snowfall, and just plain oddity. The winter of 1981–82 was particularly memorable, for it broke records in all three categories. At the time some people called it "the winter of the century," although time and subsequent winters have diminished its importance and faded its memory for many. For me, the memory is still vivid, for I spent that winter with my young family in a half-finished, half-insulated cottage, with boards and plastic in place of windows, and only a woodstove for heat. My husband still enjoys telling summertime visitors about chipping the ice out of the toilet on frigid mornings; and about how, having measured the upstairs temperature at 16°, I decided it was warm enough for a bath. Our family folklore may always include the ritual of saying "Up into the arctic!" as we climb the stairs.

Actually it wasn't so much the winter as the spring that wore us down. In mid-March we had the biggest snowstorm of the year—until the one in April. On Tuesday, April 6, twelve inches of snow fell in twenty-four hours. Two days later, while I was waiting my turn in a plumbing supply house, I overheard part of a conversation between a clerk and another customer, clearly a regular. The most popular topic for conversation that week was (of course) the weather. So after some friendly remark by the clerk, the customer replied, "I saw a robin this morning that was wearing snowshoes. He was standing outside a bait shop. (Pause) Guess he was thinking about going in to buy some worms." It snowed again on Friday, and then again on Easter Sunday.

Just as the folk still use comic elaboration to help them cope with the trials and absurdities of life, so the producers of popular culture continue to mimic oral tales. Stand-up comics exaggerate personal experiences; television specials borrow tall characters from the nineteenth century; Hal Holbrook and his imitators re-create Mark Twain's platform lectures on stage, records, and television; and every Saturday night for nearly thirteen years (1974–87), on National Public Radio, Garrison Keillor spun tall monologues about life in Lake Wobegon, Minnesota. These and other popular artists continue to spread tall fiction to a wide audience. Likewise American writers in the twentieth century have continued to portray people fantasizing, elaborating, and spinning yarns. The flush times are over, and as today's oral tall tale is often shortened by a culture more hurried and permeated by far more modes and media of communication, so the tall tale in literature is often diluted by writers who have other goals to pursue and other means to their ends. Still it persists in many forms and manifestations.

The literary incarnations of Paul Bunyan, a tall hero in at least one sense, take their subject matter but little else from the tall tale—and even how much of that subject matter comes from real folklore is uncertain. Nevertheless, these works are inspired by the idea of the American tall tale. When Paul first appeared in a lumber company promotional pamphlet (1914), the author, W.B. Laughead, may or may not have been reporting actual folktales collected from loggers; but the issue of folklore *versus* fakelore, so hotly debated by scholars, becomes a minor point in a generic study of the tall tale, where source is less important than form and intent. To the extent that Laughead's pamphlet pretends that Paul is a real person, uses the loggers' lingo, and reflects the woodsmen's values, it imitates the tall tale method and style. Laughead's later works, recast into the voice of business, separate teller from subject matter and motive from motif in such a way that the stories have little to do with tall tales. Later writers have moved Paul even further from the tall tale. James Stevens' *Paul Bunyan* is a satire, not a tall tale; and Robert Frost and Carl Sandburg, in their poetic uses of Paul, employ the motifs but not the form or the ambience of the tall tale. For them Paul is a symbol, not a character. In their work, tallness is a subject, but not a method.[1]

Tall tales told in a particular social context by fully developed characters have most often appeared in western novels in the twentieth century. Owen Wister's Virginian defeats his enemy Trampas three times: once through quiet courage at the poker table, once with a tall tale that humiliates Trampas, and finally with a gun. The Virginian is not only courageous, loyal, strong, handsome, and innately noble. He is also a humorist and master yarnspinner among the cowboys. His storytelling prowess is essential to his status as hero. In later western fiction, however, the hero has often possessed a more laconic character, using language, as John Cawelti has observed, the same way he uses his gun: as seldom as possible, but then always with precision and powerful effect.[2] Jesting and comic yarnspinning may then be taken over by secondary characters. In many of these western novels—filled as they are with romance and adventure—tall tale humor is not a pervading force or predominating mood but a trait of character, a source of comic relief, or a symbol of western wildness and exuberance.

The western novel that most closely approximates nineteenth-century tall literature is a work known mostly for being made into a popular film. Thomas Berger's novel-length frame tale, *Little Big Man* (1964), tells the narrative of Jack Crabb's improbable adventures on the frontier. Berger's frame narrator, a "literary man," closes the book with the judgment that "Jack Crabb was either the most neglected hero in the history of this country or a liar of insane proportions."[3] Though the frame and much of Jack Crabb's tale itself bespeak tall tale inspiration, long sections of the book are far from comic. In *Little Big Man*, adventure, history, pathos, and cultural documentary accompany the tall comedy—the teasing of the reader's credulity—to create an experience far more varied and complex than either a tall tale event or a nineteenth-century literary frame tale.

Novels and tales not specifically western also use yarnspinners, tall tale atmosphere, and tall tale technique. O. Henry's "Gentle Grafter," Jefferson Peters, tells outlandish but meticulously plotted tales of cons—successful and unsuccessful—to a solemnly appreciative frame narrator reminiscent of G.W. Harris' "George":

Jeff Peters must be reminded. Whenever he is called upon, pointedly, for a story, he will maintain that his life has been as devoid of incident as the longest of Trollope's novels. But lured, he will divulge. Therefore I cast many and divers flies upon the current of his thoughts before I feel a nibble.[4]

One such lure brings up a tale about trying to con a very modern farmer, and begins like this:

"One morning me and Andy wakes up with sixty-eight cents between us in a yellow pine hotel on the edge of the pre-digested hoe-cake belt of Southern Indiana. How we got off the train there the night before I can't tell you; for she went through the village so fast that what looked like a saloon to us through the car window turned out to be a composite view of a drug store and a water tank two blocks apart." (34)

O. Henry specialized in the humor of incongruity and surprise, not just in his endings, but in his humorous combinations and distortions of words: malapropisms, comic comparisons, and tall tale conceits. Though Jeff Peters apparently tells his tales as true, they have an unmistakably tall atmosphere about them.

Ring Lardner developed, in addition to many colloquial characters, an authorial persona who decorated his facts with tall humor and wrote extravagant fictions as if they were solemn facts. Through his reports of the 1922 "World Serious" runs a comic motif about the fur coat he has promised his wife if his team should win. The coat begins as a costly fur, but is reduced first to a horse skin and then to the coats of the three family kittens. At the end of the series, when his team has lost, Lardner asks his readers to tear off the plush covers from their old family albums and send them along to make his wife a plush coat.[5]

Longer and more complex works, like William Faulkner's *The Hamlet* (1931), may be enriched with multi-layered evocations of tall oral narrative. Faulkner's authorial voice — conversational, colloquial, rambling, parenthetical — ascribes tall tale self-consciousness to animals and inanimate objects by dropping swift, simple phrases in unexpected places. In Book IV of *The Hamlet*, entitled "The Peasants," one of the Spotted Horses stampedes through Mrs. Littlejohn's house. It crashes into her melodeon, the narrator tells us, producing "a single note, almost a chord, in bass, resonant and grave, of deep and sober astonishment."[6] Faulkner's characters, too, use tall tale language. When V.K. Ratliff speaks, other characters listen — not only because the traveling salesman has news from all over the county, but because his yarning style compels attention. When Ratliff asserts that Ab Snopes was "soured" by a horse-swapping deal with Pat Stamper, his audience invites him to elaborate, their grudging admiration for his breadth of knowledge tempered by skepticism:

Once more for a moment no one spoke. Then the first speaker said: "How did you find all this out? I reckon you was there, too." (p. 30)

Ratliff then tells how Ab Snopes unwittingly bought back the horse he thought he was rid of, because Stamper and his Negro accomplice had dyed the horse and pumped air under its skin with a bicycle pump, turning a bony bay horse into a plump black one. No one explicitly questions the accuracy of Ratliff's details. Whether they respond in contemplative silence or quiet laughter, they continue to listen. Retelling the story of the Spotted Horse in Mrs. Littlejohn's house, Ratliff recreates chaos with exaggeration:

"Maybe there wasn't but one of them things in Mrs. Littlejohn's house that night . . . But it was the biggest drove of just one horse that I ever seen. It was in my room and it was on the front porch and I could hear Mrs. Littlejohn hitting it over the head with that washboard all at the same time." (p. 309)

With the exception of his fantasy about Flem Snopes in hell defeating "the Prince," Ratliff's yarns are mostly anecdotes and personal narratives, intended to be believed as factual representations of actual events, but they are laced with the flavors of the tall tale.

The flavors and inspiration of the tall tale also imbue a work like Philip Roth's *The Great American Novel*. As the title suggests, the book is deliberately modeled after great American novels. Its opening and closing echo Melville: "Call me Smitty," and "The Drama's done. Why then does one step forth?—Because one did survive the wreck of the Patriot League." In his prologue the "author" notes his book's similarities to *The Scarlet Letter, Moby Dick,* and *Huckleberry Finn*.[7] And yet Roth claims that the book has no "redeeming value," save comic inventiveness. He has anchored his fantasy in particular historical facts, not, he claims, to provide a commentary on American history or culture but "to establish a kind of passageway from the imaginary that seems real to the real that seems imaginary, a continuum between the

credible incredible and the incredible credible."⁸ This is the realm
evoked by the tall tale. The breezy colloquial style, the dialogue inspired by tape-recorded recollections of professional baseball players,
the rambling lists, the punning and alliteration, and the tall imagery
also recall oral yarnspinning, sometimes brought to us by way of radio
sportscasting:

It did not take but one pitch, of course, for Mike the Mouth to become
the lifelong enemy of Gil Gamesh. Huge Crowd, sunny day, flags snapping
in the breeze. Gil winds up, kicks and here comes that long left arm,
America, around by way of the tropical Equator.⁹

For Smitty, verbal artistry provides not just an amusing pastime but an
avenue of revenge. He and his league and much of America have been
wronged, and the yarnspinner's humorous telling of the tale provides
a kind of final moral triumph.

The political importance of words, the power of the comic monologue, also rationalizes and holds together works more distantly related
to the tall tale. Ralph Ellison, apparently prompted by Constance Rourke's
American Humor to recognize the primacy of monologue in American comic tradition, created in *Invisible Man* (1952) a character whose
strength and to some extent downfall derive from his verbal talents.¹⁰
Though eloquence has long been one of black America's primary tools
for survival, Ellison uses both black and white traditions. Philip Roth,
too, uses extravagant comic monologue to search for meaning in a hos-
tile world. In *Portnoy's Complaint* (1967) the stand-up Jewish comic,
now lying down, spins off comic anecdotes to shock, manipulate, explain, and amuse.

In *Portnoy* we also begin to see the writer's interest in comic extravagance moving away from folkloric sources and toward absurdist philosophy, for in the end all of Portnoy's talk neither conquers the enemy
nor exorcises his rage. He closes with a scream of anguish. The narrative
voice in Joseph Heller's *Catch-22* also expresses madness and a feeling
of impotence. Violence and death are inescapable; there is no rational
way of understanding the army, the war, the world. So in *Catch-22* tall
humor, along with grotesquery and a scrambled narrative order, create
an extravagant comic vision which is both the only way of surviving and
the only way of describing a crazy world. The promotion-by-computer

of a character named Major Major to the rank of major, the justification of Milo Mindbinder's collaboration with the enemy on the grounds of a patriotic allegiance to the American values of profit and entrepreneurial spirit, and Orr's escape on a life raft with his over-sized cheeks full of food all push us beyond the borders of the probable and the credible and into the regions inhabited by the tall tale.

Comic absurdists have not always created such jarringly-organized novels. Nor have they always emphasized their protagonists' powerlessness in an absurd world. John Barth's comic revision of Maryland history, *The Sot-Weed Factor*, portrays a character who faces hardship and absurdity not with a scream of rage or an attempt to escape, nor yet with the traditional yarnspinner's tall tale, but with action. "Assert!" counsels the existentialist Henry Burlingame:

"One must needs make and seize his soul, and then cleave fast to 't, or go babbling in the corner; one must choose his gods and devils on the run, quill his own name upon the universe, and declare, "Tis I, and the world stands such-a-way!"" One must assert, assert, assert, or go screaming mad."[11]

Though its form is modeled after the eighteenth-century novel rather than the oral tale or the mad comic monologue, *The Sot-Weed Factor* is a grand tall tale itself—turning historical fact into extravagant fiction; drawing on and counting on the readers' collective, communal understanding of early American history; and comically, irreverently inverting the traditonal values associated with that history, to the delight of a modern audience that has partly abandoned those values. If not directly and consciously inspired by the oral tall tale, Barth nonetheless makes hilarious use of that part of his cultural and literary heritage.

More directly inspired by contemporary oral narrative, Garrison Keillor's *Lake Wobegon Days* grew out of the author's rambling radio monologues reporting "The News from Lake Wobegon." Both the monologues and the book inhabit that hazy realm between fiction that pretends to be fact and fact that pretends to be fiction. The town itself exists on no map. Keillor has, of course, a tall explanation for that oversight, explained on the radio and repeated in the book:

The Coleman survey outfit, headed by Lieutenant Michael Coleman, had been attached to Grant's army, which they misdirected time and again so that Grant's flanks kept running head-on into Lee's rear until Union officers learned to make "right face" a 120-degree turn. Governor Marshall, however, regarded the 1866 survey as preliminary—"It will provide us a good general idea of the State, a foundation upon which we can build in the future," he said—though of course it turned out to be the final word.

The map was drawn by four teams of surveyors under the direction of Finian Coleman, Michael having left for the Nebraska gold rush, who placed them at the four corners of the state and aimed them inward. The southwest and northwest contingents moved fast over level ground, while the eastern teams got bogged down in the woods, so that, when they met a little west of Lake Wobegon, the four quadrants didn't fit within the boundaries legislated by Congress in 1851. Nevertheless, Finian mailed them to St. Paul, leaving the legislature to wrestle with the discrepancy.

The legislature simply reproportioned the state by eliminating the overlap in the middle, the little quadrangle that is Mist County. "The soil of that region is unsuited to agriculture, and we doubt that its absence would be much noticed," Speaker of the House Randolph remarked.

In 1933, a legislative interim commission proposed that the state recover the lost county by collapsing the square mileage of several large lakes. The area could be removed from the centers of the lakes, elongating them slightly so as not to lose valuable shoreline. Opposition was spearheaded by the Bureau of Fisheries, which pointed out the walleye breeding grounds to be lost; and the State Map Amendment was attached as a rider to a bill requiring the instruction of evolution in all secondary schools and was defeated by voice vote.[12]

In the book, descriptions of the town, its history, its inhabitants, and its effect on those who leave are all presented in a sensually rich and comfortable colloquial style which echoes Keillor's voice on the radio:

It is a quiet town, where much of the day you could stand in the middle of Main Street and not be in anyone's way—not forever, but for as long as a person would want to stand in the middle of a street.

Occasionally the story, like the town, drones and begins almost to sleep, but then a humorous anecdote livens things up. In the middle of a rather dull discussion of the town siren which announces the time twice a day, he places a tall tale about his great-grandfather, who had lived all his life telling time by the sun. When his house burned down and they built a new one facing west instead of south, he became confused. "He lived in a twilight world for some time and then moved in his mind to the house he'd grown up in, and in the end didn't know one day from another until the day he died. . . . Not even the siren could have saved my great-grandpa. He died of misdirection" (p. 143).

Despite the occasional tall comedy, the pervading tone of the book is a peculiar mixture of warm nostalgia and harsh condescension. The chapter entitled "News" most directly juxtaposes these two moods. The body of the chapter contains a gently humorous discussion of the courtly formality of the local newspaper; an affectionate description of the intrusive but well-intentioned telephone operator, Elizabeth; and an admiring portrait of the narrator's grandfather—a man so upright and "so admired that when the preacher at his funeral chose the text 'For all have sinned and come short of the glory of God,' his neighbors considered it an insult." And yet in a footnote that runs the entire length of the chapter, he prints the "95 Theses" written by a former Wobegonian as a bitter complaint against the rigid mediocrity of his upbringing. The narrator attempts to reconcile these two conflicting moods by demonstrating that, while Lake Wobegon is narrow, rigid, backward, and in some ways stifling, it contains a richness of heritage and feeling just as real and just as valuable as what he finds in more progressive parts of the world.

As Keillor describes the strengths and weaknesses of a disappearing culture, a profusion of detail and a haze of nostalgia make its dullness picturesque. In this the book resembles nineteenth-century local color perhaps more than the literary tall tale. But by placing his material in the form of factual reminiscence, Keillor assumes a tall tale stance. Although he does not aggressively bait his readers in a tall tale interplay, and although there is little in the book that is really outrageous, he does ask us to sit back and follow his sometimes tall yarn wherever it might lead, as imagination and memory mingle and wander over Mist County.

As the layers of literary and cultural allusion increase in the twentieth century, the tall tale becomes a less obvious influence. If the rustic with his feet propped on the stove, spinning tall yarns in a leisurely fashion, has become rare, his progeny nonetheless find other ways to express their delight in tall humor. Whether it appears in the person of a fictional ball player, con man, or sewing machine salesman, or, more often, in the consciousness and organization of an authorial voice, comic extravagance and tall tale techniques are still with us. They come to us by way of the nineteenth-century tall tale writers, but they also echo the continuing tendency toward tall humor in our culture. The flush times may be over; but, like Barth's existentialists or Faulkner's peasants, the literary tall tale continues to assert and endure, and will as long as folk yarnspinners, whether to assert or to endure or simply to amuse, continue to spin tall tales.

On the homefront, we try to laugh at past trials and absurdities, and we look forward to each coming winter with hope and more insulation.

Notes

Preface

1. See Richard Bauman and Joel Sherzer, eds. *Exploration in the Ethnography of Speaking* (New York: Cambridge Univ. Press, 1974), "Introduction."

2. Dan Ben-Amos, "Toward a Definition of Folklore in Context," in *Toward New Perspectives in Folklore*, ed. Americo Paredes and Richard Bauman, Publication of the American Folklore Society, Bibliographical and Special Series Vol. 23 (Austin: Univ. of Texas Press, 1972), 10. See also Robert Georges, "Towards an Understanding of Storytelling Events," *Journal of American Folklore*, 82 (1969), 313–28.

3. See, for example, Alan Dundes, "The Study of Folklore in Literature and Culture," *Journal of American Folklore*, 78 (1965), 136–42.

4. See, for example, Walter Slatoff, *With Respect to Readers: Dimensions of Literary Response* (Ithaca: Cornell Univ. Press, 1970); and Walter J. Ong, S.J., "The Writer's Audience is Always a Fiction," *PMLA*, 90 (1975), 9–21.

5. Sandra K.D. Stahl, "Studying Folklore in American Literature," in *Handbook of American Folklore*, ed. Richard M. Dorson (Bloomington: Indiana Univ. Press, 1983), 429. See also Roger D. Abrahams, "Folklore and Literature as Performance," *Journal of the Folklore Institute*, 9 (1972), 75–94. Other folklorist-critics have, like me, complained about item-centered approaches to the study of folklore in literature and have moved in similar directions: see Daniel R. Barnes, "Toward the Establishment of Principles for the Study of Folklore and Literature," *Southern Folklore Quarterly*, 43 (1979), 5–16. David H. Stanley, "The Personal Narrative and the Personal Novel: Folklore as Frame and Structure for Literature," *Southern Folklore Quarterly*, 43 (1979), 107–20.

Chapter 1

1. I interviewed Don Lewis at the Royal Ambassador Camp in the summer of 1978, and at that time collected the tales and commentary that appear here and in ch. II.

2. For a more detailed discussion of the history and probable causes of exaggeration in early American humor, see Walter Blair and Hamlin Hill, *America's Humor* (New York: Oxford Press, 1978), ch. I.

3. Walter Blair quotes an 1838 review in *The London and Westminster Review* which stated that "The curiosity of the public regarding the peculiar nature of American humour seems to have been easily satisfied with the application of the all-sufficing word exaggeration," in *Native American Humor* (1937; rpt. New York: Chandler, 1960), 5. See also Max Eastman, *The Enjoyment of Laughter* (New York, 1963).

4. See Andrew Lang, "Western Drolls" in *Lost Leaders* (London, 1889), 186–87; John Neal, "Story-Telling," *New York Mirror*, 16 (April 6, 1839), 321.

5. Blair and Hill, 98.

6. Neville's article was first published in *The Western Souvenir* for 1828; it has been reprinted in Walter Blair and Franklin J. Meine, *Half Horse Half Alligator: The Growth of the Mike Fink Legend* (Chicago: Univ. of Chicago Press, 1956), 43–55.

7. See Blair and Meine, 17.

8. William T. Porter, ed., *The Big Bear of Arkansas, and Other Tales* (1843; facsimile rpt. New York: AMS Press, 1973); T.A. Burke, ed., *"Polly Peablossom's Wedding" and Other Tales* Philadelphia: T.B. Peters and Brothers, 1851); T.C. Haliburton, ed., *Traits of American Humor* 3 vols. (London: Colburn and Co., 1852) and *The Americans at Home* 2 vols. (London: Hurst & Blackett, 1854).

9. For the history of the *Spirit* see Norris W. Yates, *William T. Porter and the Spirit of the Times* (Baton Rouge: Louisiana State Univ. Press, 1957).

10. See Edmund Wilson, *Patriotic Gore: Studies in the Literature of the American Civil War* (New York: Oxford Univ. Press, 1962).

11. Yates, *William T. Porter*, 162–63. For an account of Black Harris' connection with petrified forest tales see Richard M. Dorson, *Man and Beast in American Comic Legend* (Bloomington: Indiana Univ. Press, 1982), 91–96.

12. James Hall, *Letters from the West* (1828; rpt. Gainesville, Fla.: Scholars' Facsimiles & Reprints, 1967), 346–48.

13. James Kirke Paulding, *The Lion of the West*, rev. John Augustus Stone and William Bayle Bernard, ed. James N. Tidwell (Stanford, Calif.: Stanford Univ. Press, 1954), 35–36.

14. Vance Randolph, *We Always Lie to Strangers* (New York: Columbia Univ. Press, 1951), 253–54. Roger Welsch reports a similar tale in *Shingling the Fog and Other Plains Lies* (Chicago: Swallow Press, 1972), 50.

15. Bill Davidson, *Tall Tales They Tell in the Services* (New York: Thomas Y. Crowell, 1943), 47.

Chapter 2

1. Hiram Chittenden, *The Yellowstone National Park: Historical and Descriptive* (1895; rpt. Norman: Univ. of Oklahoma Press, 1964), 49.

2. Motifs X1402.1 and X1122.4.1 in Ernest W. Baughman, *Type and Motif-Index of the Folktales of England and North America* (Bloomington: Indiana Folklore Series No. 20, 1966).

3. This particular schema was outlined by Professor Charles Perdue of the University of Virginia. Other folklorists have worked out similar classifications for folktales. See, for example, William Bascom, "The Forms of Folklore: Prose Narratives," *Journal of American Folklore*, 78 (1965), 3–20.

4. Sandra K.D. Stahl, "Introduction," *Journal of the Folklore Institute*, 14 (1977), 6.

5. Plutarch, *Moralia*, trans. Frank Cole Babbitt (1927; rpt. Cambridge, Mass.: Harvard Univ. Press, 1949), I, 79, p. 421. Plutarch probably refers to Antiphanes the Younger, who died *circa* A.D. 120.

6. Count Baldesar Castiglione, *The Book of the Courtier* trans. Leonard E. Opdycke (New York: Scribner's, 1903), II:55, 132–33.

7. Welsch, *Shingling the Fog and Other Plains Lies*, 29.

8. Gerald Thomas, *The Tall Tale and Philippe d'Alcripe: An Analysis of the Tall Tale Genre with Particular Reference to Philippe d'Alcripe's "La Nouvelle Fabrique des Excellents Traits de Verité," Together with an Annotated Translation of the Work* (St. John's, Newfoundland: Memorial Univ. of Newfoundland Folklore and Language Publication Series, Monograph Series, no. 1; Bibliographic and Special Series, vol. 29, 1977), 26–27.

9. R.E. Raspe et al., *The Singular Travels, Campaigns, and Adventures of Baron Münchausen by R.E. Raspe and Others*, ed. John Carswell (1948; rpt. New York: Dover Publications, 1960), xxvii–xxx.

10. Blair and Hill, *America's Humor*, 131.

11. Harold W. Thompson and Henry Seidel Canby, "Humor," *Literary History of the United States*, ed. Robert E. Spiller et al., rev. ed. (New York: Macmillan, 1957), 728.

12. Gustav Hennigsen, "The Art of Perpendicular Lying, Concerning a

Commercial Collecting of Norwegian Sailors' Tall Tales," trans. Warren E. Roberts, *Journal of the Folklore Institute*, 2 (1965).

13. Baughman, xxi, xvii.

14. Roger Welsch reports a readers' column entitled "The Liars Lair" which ran in the *Nebraska Farmer* between December 6, 1924, and May 16, 1925, and was subtitled "A Prize Contest to Determine Who is the Champion Liar of Nebraska." The winner of the contest was a woman, but she presented her tale as having been told by a male relative. Evidently, tall yarning is something that men do, but writing to newspaper columns is something that women do.

15. George N. Gage et al., *History of Washington, New Hampshire* (Claremont, N.H., 1886), 67, quoted in Richard M. Dorson, *Jonathan Draws the Long Bow* (Cambridge, Mass.: Harvard Univ. Press, 1946), 6.

16. Antii Aarne, *The Types of the Folktale; a Classification and Bibliography*, trans. and enlarged by Stith Thompson, 2nd rev. ed., F.F. Communications, No. 3 (Helsinki: Suomalainen Tiedeakatemia, 1964), F.F. Communications v. 75, no. 184. This work was originally published by Aarne in 1910 and first revised by Thompson in 1928.

17. William Hugh Jansen, *Abraham "Oregon" Smith: Pioneer, Folk Hero, and Tale-Teller* (New York: Arno Press, 1977). Jansen's book was originally a doctoral diss., Indiana Univ., 1949.

18. Mody C. Boatright, *Gib Morgan, Minstrel of the Oil Fields*, Texas Folklore Society Publication no. 20 (El Paso: Texas Folklore Society, 1945), 5.

19. Mody C. Boatright, *Folk Laughter on the American Frontier* (1942; rpt. New York: Macmillan, 1949), 87.

20. Richard K. Lunt, "Jones Tracy—Tall-Tale Hero from Mount Desert Island," *Northeast Folklore*, 10 (1968), 65–66.

21. Herbert Halpert, "John Darling, a New York Munchausen," *Journal of American Folklore*, 57 (1944), 98–99.

22. Vance Randolph, *We Always Lie to Strangers*, 7.

23. Kay Lorraine Cothran, "Such Stuff as Dreams: A Folkloristic Sociology of Fantasy in the Okefenokee Rim, Georgia," Diss. Univ. of Pennsylvania, 1972.

24. Patrick B. Mullen, *I Heard the Old Fisherman Say: Folklore of the Texas Gulf Coast* (Austin: Univ. of Texas Press, 1978).

25. Alan Dundes breaks down the analysis of folktales into three parts: texture, text, and context. For the present discussion, "text" includes such textural elements as rhythm, onomatopoeia, alliteration, and stress. See Alan Dundes, "Texture, Text, and Context," *Southern Folklore Quarterly*, 28 (1964), 251–65.

26. Boatright, *Gib Morgan*, 48.

27. Jansen, 168–69; supported by other informants, 167. The parenthetical remark is Jansen's.

28. Norman Studer reports another summer camp storyteller who empha-

sizes the humor of his tales. Mike Todd, a former rafter, bark-peeler, guide, bear hunter, and fire observer hired as "resident folklorist" at Camp Woodland "loves children and enjoys telling them stories. His own hearty laugh punctuates every tale. He jokingly refers to himself as the 'biggest liar in Ulster County.' " Norman Studer, "Yarns of a Catskill Woodsman," *New York Folklore Quarterly*, 11 (1955), 184.

29. See William Labov and Joshua Waletzky, "Narrative Analysis: Oral Versions of Personal Experience," *Essays on the Verbal and Visual Arts*, ed. June Helm (Seattle: Proceedings of the 1966 Annual Spring Meeting of the American Ethnological Society), 12–44.

30. Barre Toelken, *The Dynamics of Folklore* (Boston: Houghton Mifflin, 1979), 112.

31. The literary works with which I will be concerned in later chapters are largely patterned after the narrative tall tales. The use of the term "tall tale" will then, therefore, be quite appropriate.

32. Bascom, 6.

33. From a tape recording made by Professor Kenneth S. Goldstein, Dept. of Folklore and Folklife, Univ. of Pennsylvania, copy in the possession of Charles L. Perdue, Jr., Dept. of English, Univ. of Virginia.

34. Jansen, 209.

35. Boatright, *Folk Laughter*, 93.

36. Welsch, 82–83 (Nebraska); Randolph, 120–21 (Missouri); Stith Thompson, *The Folktale* (1946; rpt. Berkeley: Univ. of California Press, 1977), 214 (Europe).

37. Chittenden, 49–50.

38. Gilbert Ryle, *The Concept of Mind* (New York: Barnes & Noble, n.d. [1950?]). Ryle offers only one humorous example of a category mistake: "She came home in a flood of tears and a sedan-chair." The category mistake here is created by conjoining adjectival and adverbial phrases using the single preposition "in." In their motif indexes, Stith Thompson and Ernest Baughman label motifs X1700–1799, "Lying tales based on absurd logic or the lack of logic." They seem, however, to have a rather hazy notion of this category, since many of the motifs they place in it are no more absurdly illogical than the ordinary lies of exaggeration which they exclude. My discussion of illogical exaggeration is not intended to be based on their motif classification.

39. Welsch, 20.

40. Gene Caesar, *King of the Mountain Men: The Life of Jim Bridger* (New York: Dutton, 1961), 14.

41. Recorded in a private interview at the National Council for the Traditional Arts' National Folk Festival, in Vienna, Virginia, 1978. Van Holyoak died in a traffic accident in the summer of 1980, while this manuscript was in preparation.

42. Randolph, 105.

43. Welsch, 16.

44. Randolph, 153.

45. Brunhilde Biebuyck-Goetz, "'This is the Dyin' Truth': Mechanisms of Lying," *Journal of the Folklore Institute*, 14 (1977), 78–79.

46. Biebuyck-Goetz never goes quite this far. She does, however, stress the need for further study of the relationship between personal narratives and other genres: "Personal experience has been instrumental in the Ray brothers' tales as material upon which they build narratives, and as a performance model for lies, which they make believable by emulating the delivery of personal stories," 80.

47. See, for example, Northrop Frye's essay on the theory of genres in *Anatomy of Criticism: Four Essays* (Princeton, N.J.: Princeton Univ. Press, 1957), especially 247.

48. Morton L. Gurewitch, *Comedy: The Irrational Vision* (Ithaca: Cornell Univ. Press, 1975), 9–10.

49. Sandra K.D. Stahl, "Style in Oral and Written Narrative," *Southern Folklore Quarterly*, 43 (1979), 50–53.

50. Abrahams, "Folklore and Literature as Performance," 78.

51. Cothran, 192, et passim.

52. Herbert Halpert, "Tall Tales and Other Yarns from Calgary, Alberta," *California Folklore Quarterly*, 4 (1945), 32.

53. Lunt, 39.

54. Welsch, 11.

55. Halpert, "Calgary," 32.

56. Kenneth Burke, "Literature as Equipment for Living," in *The Philosophy of Literary Form: Studies in Symbolic Action* (1941; rpt. Baton Rouge: Louisiana State Univ. Press, 1967).

57. Toelken, 51.

58. Kenneth Boulding used the idea of a value image in his definition of a subculture, in *The Image: Knowledge in Life and Society* (Ann Arbor: Univ. of Michigan Press, 1956), 133, 143.

59. Kay L. Cothran, "Talking Trash in the Okefenokee Swamp Rim, Georgia," *Journal of American Folklore*, 87 (1974), 353.

60. Halpert, "John Darling," 98–99.

61. Jansen, 160–61.

62. Robert Scholes, *Structuralism in Literature* (New Haven: Yale Univ. Press, 1974), 47.

63. Jansen, 164, 166.

Chapter 3

1. *William Byrd's Histories of the Dividing Line Betwixt Virginia and North Carolina*, ed. William K. Boyd (New York: Dover, 1967). See, for example, p. 54 and pp. 90-92.

2. Letter in the *Public Advertiser*, May 22, 1765, rpt. in *Benjamin Franklin's Letters to the Press, 1758-1775*, ed. Verner W. Crane (Chapel Hill: Univ. of North Carolina Press, 1950), 33-34.

3. Christian Schultz, Jr., *Travels on a Inland Voyage through the Territories of Indiana, Louisiana, Mississippi and New Orleans, Performed in the Years 1807 and 1808* (1810; facsimile rpt. University Microfilms, 1979), II, 145.

4. John Donald Wade, *Augustus Baldwin Longstreet: A Study of the Development of Culture in the South* (New York: Macmillan, 1924), 149-56.

5. Ibid., 150.

6. Edgar Allan Poe was probably the first critic to point out Longstreet's debt to the *Spectator*, in his highly complimentary review of *Georgia Scenes* in the *Southern Literary Messenger*, 2 (1836), 287-92.

7. Augustus Baldwin Longstreet, *Georgia Scenes: Characters, Incidents, &c, in the First Half Century of the Republic by a Native Georgian*, 2nd ed. (New York: Harper, 1840), 129. Parenthetical references will be to this edition.

8. Quoted by Lewis O. Saum in *The Popular Mood of Pre-Civil War America*, Contributions in American Studies, 46 (Westport, Conn.: Greenwood Press, 1980), 171.

9. Mark Twain, *The Adventures of Huckleberry Finn*, ed. Scully Bradley et al. (New York: Norton, 1961), 113.

10. Wade, 148.

11. For a discussion of actual "rough and tumble" fighting in the Old Southwest see Elliot Gorn, "'Gouge and Bite, Pull Hair and Scratch': The Social Significance of Fighting in the Southern Backcountry," *American Historical Review*, 90 (1985), 18-43. According to Gorn, "Foreign travelers might exaggerate and backwoods storytellers embellish, but the most neglected fact about eye-gouging matches is their actuality" (33).

12. William L. Hedges, *Washington Irving: An American Study, 1802-1832* (Baltimore: Johns Hopkins Press, 1965), 98, 105, 146, 157-58.

13. According to Richard M. Dorson, the Crockett almanacs were "first published in Nashville, then in New York and Boston as their fame spread; Philadelphia, Albany, Baltimore, and Louisville imprints attest their popularity." *Davy Crockett, American Comic Legend* (New York: Rockland Editions, 1939), iv.

14. Dorson, ibid., 16. Because only scattered copies of the almanacs are

available in rare book rooms, my quotations will all be from Dorson's readily available anthology. This particular tale can also be found in Walter Blair's *Native American Humor*, 285–86.

15. According to Benjamin Perley Poore, *Perley's Reminiscences of Sixty Years in the National Metropolis*, cited in James N. Tidwell's introduction to Paulding's *The Lion of the West*.

16. For reliable biographical information and a discussion of the relationship between Crockett's biographies and his political career, see the introduction and notes to *A Narrative of the Life of David Crockett of the State of Tennessee*, ed. and intro. James A. Shackford and Stanley J. Folmsbee (1834; facsimile rpt. Knoxville: Univ. of Tennessee Press, 1973).

17. A copy of Fisher & Brother's 1852 *Crockett Almanac* is held in the Barrett Collection at the University of Virginia along with variously titled Crockett almanacs for 1843, 1844, 1845, and 1850.

18. *The Spirit of the Times*, 4 Nov. 1843, p. 426. More detailed discussions of Stewart's expedition and the Field and Thorpe letters can be found in Milton Rickels, *Thomas Bangs Thorpe, Humorist of the Old Southwest* (Baton Rouge: Louisiana State Univ. Press, 1962), 77–86.

19. According to Rickels, only two of Thorpe's letters are available in extant copies of the *Intelligencer*. Like him, I have used the letters as reprinted in the *Spirit*. Parenthetical citations refer to dates and pages in the *Spirit*.

20. *Spirit*, 13 Jan. 1844, p. 546; five of Field's thirty-nine letters appeared in the *Spirit*, according to Yates, *William T. Porter and the Spirit*, 169.

21. Mark Twain, "The Petrified Man," in *The Works of Mark Twain*, XV, *Early Tales and Sketches Vol. I(1851–64)*, ed. Edgar Marquess Branch and Robert H. Hirst (Berkeley: Iowa Center for Textual Studies, Univ. of California Press, 1979), 159.

22. "A Couple of Sad Experiences," *Galaxy*, 9 (1870), 858–61. Most of the essay was reprinted in *Sketches New and Old*, 1875.

23. DeLancy Ferguson, "The Petrified Truth," *The Colophon*, 2 (1937), 189–96.

24. Stephen Fender has briefly discussed the need for "some element of self-falsification" in "'The Prodigal in a Far Country of Chawing Husks': Mark Twain's Search for a Style in the West," *Modern Language Review*, 71 (1976), 737–56.

25. *Early Tales and Sketches*, 324.

26. See *Early Tales and Sketches*, 320–23, and Richard C. Lillard, "Contemporary Reaction to 'The Empire City Massacre,'" *American Literature*, 16 (1944), 198–203.

27. Walter Blair and Hamlin Hill list people fooled by him in *America's Humor*, 246–47. Ferguson finds no evidence that the "Solar Armor" or "Travelling Stones" hoaxes were reprinted as factual reporting.

28. William Wright (Dan DeQuille) as quoted in C. Grant Loomis, "The Tall Tales of Dan DeQuille," *California Folklore Quarterly*, 5 (1946), 33–34.

29. Kenneth S. Lynn, *Mark Twain and Southwest Humor* (Boston: Little, Brown, 1959).

30. William C. Hall, "How Sally Hooter Got Snake Bit," in *Humor of the Old Southwest*, ed. Hennig Cohen and William B. Dillingham (Boston: Houghton Mifflin, 1964).

31. "Where Joe Meriweather Went To," in *"Polly Peablossom's Wedding" and Other Tales*, ed. Burke.

32. "The Trapper's Story" in *The Americans at Home*, ed. Haliburton, II, 257–70.

33. The definitive discussion of the unreliable narrator in fiction is in Wayne C. Booth's *The Rhetoric of Fiction* (1961; rpt. Chicago: Univ. of Chicago Press, 1983); for a specific mention of collusion between author and reader see p. 304.

34. Although I disagree with Kenneth Lynn's interpretation of *Georgia Scenes* (for he takes the frame narrator entirely "straight"), my reading of "The Big Bear" closely parallels his, and I am indebted to his book for many insights into the sketch.

35. T.B. Thorpe, "The Big Bear of Arkansas" in *The Big Bear of Arkansas, and Other Tales*, ed. William T. Porter, 13–31. All parenthetical references will be to this edition.

36. Linda Degh, "Folk Narrative," in *Folklore and Folklife, An Introduction*, ed. Richard M. Dorson (Chicago: Univ. of Chicago Press, 1972), 72–74.

37. Three tales in which Mike Hooter is the narrator appear anonymously in *"Polly Peablossom's Wedding" and Other Tales*.

38. Mikhail Bakhtin, *Rabelais and His World*, trans. Helene Iswolsky (Cambridge, Mass.: MIT Press, 1968), 19–20.

39. Ibid., 50.

40. Milton Rickels, "The Grotesque Body of Southwestern Humor," in *Critical Essays on American Humor*, ed. W. Bedford Clark and W. Craig Turner (Boston: G.K. Hall, 1984), 164. My discussion of this scene is largely based upon suggestions from Mr. Rickels.

41. "The Way Billy Harris Drove the Drum-Fish to Market," in *Traits of American Humor*, ed. T.C. Haliburton, I, 262–63.

Chapter 4

1. Edmund Wilson, *Patriotic Gore*, 509.

2. Franklin Meine, ed., *Tall Tales of the Southwest* (New York: Knopf, 1930), xxiv.

3. Two other critics have discussed Sut's stories as fiction. See Robert Micklus, "Sut's Travels with Dad," *Studies in American Humor*, 1, New Series (1982), 89–101; and Noel Polk, "The Blind Bull, Human Nature: Sut Lovingood and the Damned Human Race," in *Gyascutus: Studies in Antebellum Southern Humorous and Sporting Writing*, ed. James L.W. West III. *Costerus: Essays in English and American Language and Literature*, New Series Vols. V–VI (Atlantic Highlands, N.J.: Humanities Press, 1978), 13–49.

4. Mark Twain, *Roughing It*, Chapter LIII. This story was also told many times on the lecture platform and retold in the *Autobiography*. See *Mark Twain in Eruption*, ed. Bernard DeVoto (1922; rpt. New York: Harper & Brothers, 1940), 217–24.

5. George W. Harris, *Sut Lovingood. Yarns Spun by a "Nat'ral Born Durn'd Fool." Warped and Wove for Public Wear* (New York: Fitzgerald Publishing Corporation, 1867). All future references will be to this edition, with page numbers appearing in the text. The first Sut story, "Sut Lovingood's Daddy, Acting Horse," appeared in the *Spirit of the Times* in November 1854. Until his death in 1869, Harris continued writing about Sut and planned a second collection of his works which was lost in manuscript at the time of his death. The uncollected works were finally edited by Thomas Inge and issued under the title *High Times and Hard Times* (Nashville, Tenn.: Vanderbilt Univ. Press, 1967). Selections from the *Yarns* have been reprinted in Meine's *Tall Tales of the Southwest* and in Walter Blair, *Native American Humor*.

6. Kay L. Cothran, "Talking Trash in the Okefenokee Swamp Rim, Georgia," 348.

7. Milton Rickels, *George Washington Harris* (New York: Twayne Publishers, 1965), 80–81, 139.

8. Reprinted in Walter Blair and Franklin J. Meine, *Half Horse Half Alligator*, 220–25; for the motif's history see Richard Dorson, "The Jonny-Cake Papers," *Journal of American Folklore*, 58 (1945), 107 and D.M. McKeithan, "Bull Rides Described by 'Scroggins,' G.W. Harris, and Mark Twain," *Southern Folklore Quarterly*, 17 (1953), 241–43.

9. Enid Welsford, *The Fool: His Social and Literary History* (London: Faber and Faber, 1935), 3.

10. Ibid., 55.

11. Kay L. Cothran, "Such Stuff as Dreams," 198. In this particular society, the storyteller's social deviance includes resistance to progress and upward mobility. In other places and other times, the middle and upper classes have their own yarnspinners.

12. Welsford, 50–51. Walter Blair was perhaps the first to point out the similarity between Sut and Eulenspiegel as described by Enid Welsford; see Blair, *Native American Humor*, 101. Milton Rickels suggests that one of Sut's

functions and part of his appeal consist in the fool's creation of the illusion of freedom, in *George Washington Harris*, 102–103.

Chapter 5

1. Fred W. Lorch, *The Trouble Begins at Eight: Mark Twain's Lecture Tours* (Ames: Iowa State Univ. Press, 1968), 285.

2. Mark Twain, *Roughing It*, in *The Works of Mark Twain*, Vol. II, ed. Franklin R. Rogers and Paul Baender (Berkeley: Iowa Center for Textual Studies, Univ. of California Press, 1972), 43. All future references to *Roughing It* will be to this edition, with page numbers inserted parenthetically in the text.

3. That some such transformation occurred in fact is suggested by Stephen Fender, who compares Mark Twain's letters home during his early trip east with the letters written from Nevada and California. Fender finds in the eastern letters a reverence for tradition and historic associations. The western letters display a new ironic treatment of traditional culture and values, inspired, Fender argues, by the extreme contrasts and tensions of the West. See Fender, "'The Prodigal in a Far Country of Chawing Husks,'" 737–56.

4. Official reports of this incident record no survivors (see notes on *Roughing It*, Rogers and Baender, 556); Mark Twain may, nevertheless, have believed the tradition. The amazing wanderings of such survivors are recorded in biographies of mountain men like Hugh Glass and Jim Bridger. Winfred Blevins collected these strange tales, some of which are probably true, in *Give Your Heart to the Hawks* (1973; rpt. Chicago: Avon Books, 1976).

5. James M. Cox, *Mark Twain: The Fate of Humor* (Princeton, N.J.: Princeton Univ. Press, 1966), 103.

6. Henry Nash Smith is particularly lucid in his discussion of the "Lost in the Snow" episode. See *Mark Twain: The Development of a Writer* (1962; rpt. New York: Atheneum, 1972), 56–59.

7. Left with the possibility that his story might be entirely factual, biographers and critics have searched in vain for these records. See, for example, Albert Bigelow Paine, *Mark Twain: A Biography* (New York: Harper, 1912), Vol. I, 201–202, and Rogers and Baender, note on *Roughing It*, 583.

8. "How to Tell a Story," originally published in *Youth's Companion*, October 3, 1895, rpt. in *Selected Shorter Writings of Mark Twain*, ed. Walter Blair (Boston: Houghton Mifflin, 1962), 240.

Chapter 6

1. Mark Twain, *Mark Twain's Autobiography*, ed. Albert Bigelow Paine (New York: Harper & Brothers, 1924), I, xv. No complete edition of Mark Twain's *Autobiography* has yet been published. Paine's version has been followed by two others: *Mark Twain in Eruption*, ed. Bernard DeVoto, and *The Autobiography of Mark Twain*, ed. Charles Neider (New York: Harper & Row, 1959). According to DeVoto, Paine published "something less than half of the typescript in which everything that Mark wanted in his memoirs had been brought together. This book [DeVoto's] uses about half of the remainder" (p. vii). Paine's edition uses some of Mark Twain's early written autobiography, but concentrates on the autobiographical dictations of 1906. He omits the more strident passages about Mark Twain's contemporaries. DeVoto's edition, subtitled *Hitherto Unpublished Pages About Men and Events*, concentrates on the people, politics, and philosophies of Mark Twain's later years. Neider, wishing to publish a popular version of the *Autobiography*, ignored the author's instructions that the material be printed in the free-association order in which it was written, and arranged the material chronologically, beginning with Mark Twain's birth and ending with the death of Jean Clemens in 1909. He claims to have included "30,000 or 40,000 words which have never before seen print" (p. ix), but because of his radical rearrangements it is difficult to determine which of the material is new. A complete edition of the material which Mark Twain designated as belonging in his *Autobiography* is currently being prepared at the University of California, Berkeley.

I have taken material from the three available editions and have cited my sources parenthetically in the text.

2. Kay L. Cothran, "Such Stuff as Dreams," 213.

3. "To Howells," 17 April 1909, *Selected Mark Twain*–Howells Letters, ed. Frederick Anderson et al. (New York: Atheneum, 1968), 401–402.

4. Bernard DeVoto has claimed that the impulse to write the *Autobiography* was in part the same as the impulse that inspired *What is Man?* and *The Mysterious Stranger:* "They are an interpretation of personal tragedy, a confession of guilt, a plea for understanding and pardon, a defiance of fate, and a judgment passed on mankind and its place in the universe" (DeVoto, xx–xxi). DeVoto believes that the autobiographical impulse "was arrested short of genuine self-revelation because the 'uncrystalized but enveloping dread' was so central in him that he could approach it only symbolically, by way of fiction" (xvii)—but not often, one must add, by way of humorous tall tale fiction. I see the autobiographical impulse as much more joyous—a celebration of character more than a revelation, confession, judgment, or plea for pardon.

5. Walter Blair and Hamlin Hill borrowed the notion of eiron and alazon from Aristotle and applied it to American humor in *America's Humor*, 128–29.

6. "To Mary Fairbanks," 5 October 1868, *Mark Twain to Mrs. Fairbanks*, ed. Dixon Wector (San Marino, Calif,: Huntington Library, 1949), 39–40.

7. "Letter to Howells," Anderson, 388.

8. Albert Bigelow Paine, *Mark Twain: A Biography*, II, 743–44 and IV, 1321.

9. William Dean Howells, "Mark Twain: An Inquiry," originally published in *The North American Review*, Feb. 1901; rpt. *My Mark Twain: Reminiscences and Criticisms*, ed. Marilyn Austin Baldwin (Baton Rouge: Louisiana State Univ. Press, 1967), 158.

Chapter 7

1. Reprinted as "Crockett's Coon Story," in Walter Blair, *Native American Humor*, 281–82.

2. Mark Twain, "The Notorious Jumping Frog of Calaveras County," in *Selected Shorter Writings of Mark Twain*, ed. Walter Blair, 14.

3. Ibid., 13.

4. Mark Twain, *Roughing It*, in *The Works of Mark Twain*, Vol. II, ed. Franklin R. Rogers and Paul Baender, 391.

5. Richard Bridgman, *The Colloquial Style in America* (New York: Oxford Univ. Press, 1966), 12.

Epilogue

1. For a collection of Paul Bunyan literature, see Daniel G. Hoffman, *Paul Bunyan, Last of the Frontier Demigods* (Philadelphia: Univ. of Pennsylvania Press for Temple Univ. Publications, 1952; rpt. New York: Columbia Univ. Press, 1966). For the debate on sources, see Richard M. Dorson, *Folklore and Fakelore: Essays Toward a Discipline of Folk Studies* (Cambridge, Mass.: Harvard Univ. Press, 1976); Jan Harold Brunvand, *The Study of American Folklore* (New York: Norton, 1968), 2, 92; Constance Rourke, "Paul Bunyan," *New Republic*, 23 (1920), 176–79; and Edith Fowke, "In Defense of Paul Bunyan," *New York Folklore*, 5 (1979), 43–51.

2. John G. Cawelti, *The Six-Gun Mystique* (Bowling Green, Ohio: Bowling Green Univ. Popular Press, 1984), 61.

3. Thomas Berger, *Little Big Man* (New York: Dial Press, 1964), 440.

4. O. Henry (William Sydney Porter), *The Gentle Grafter* (1904; rpt. New York: Doubleday, Page, 1916), 33.

5. Ring Lardner, "A World Serious," in *The Portable Ring Lardner*, ed. Gilbert Seldes (New York: Viking Press, 1946).

6. William Faulkner, *The Hamlet* (1931; rpt. New York: Random House, 1964), 302–303.

7. Philip Roth, *The Great American Novel* (New York: Holt, Rinehart and Winston, 1973).

8. Philip Roth, "Reading Myself," *Partisan Review* 40 (1973), 404–17.

9. Roth, *Novel*, 59.

10. Alfred Kazin, *Bright Book of Life: American Novelists and Storytellers from Hemingway to Mailer* (1971; rpt. Notre Dame: Univ. of Notre Dame Press, 1980), 247.

11. John Barth, *The Sot-Weed Factor* (1960; rpt. New York: Bantam Books, 1969), 373.

12. Garrison Keillor, *Lake Wobegon Days* (New York: Viking, 1985), 91.

Bibliography

Primary Sources

Baldwin, Joseph G. *The Flush Times of Alabama and Mississippi: a Series of Sketches.* 1853; rpt. New York: D. Appleton, 1861.

Barth, John. *The Sot-Weed Factor.* 1960; rpt. New York: Bantam Books, 1969.

Berger, Thomas. *Little Big Man.* New York: Dial Press, 1964.

Blevins, Winfred. *Give Your Heart to the Hawks.* 1973; rpt. Chicago: Avon Books, 1976.

Burke, T.A., ed. *"Polly Peablossom's Wedding" and Other Tales.* Philadelphia: T.B. Peters and Brothers, 1851.

Byrd, William. *William Byrd's Histories of the Dividing Line Betwixt Virginia and North Carolina.* Ed. William K. Boyd. New York: Dover, 1967.

Castiglione, Count Baldesar. *The Book of the Courtier.* Trans. Leonard E. Opdycke. New York: Scribner's, 1903.

Clemens, Samuel Langhorne (Mark Twain). *The Adventures of Thomas Jefferson Snodgrass.* Ed. Charles Honce. Chicago, 1928; rpt. Folcroft, Pa.: Folcroft Press, 1969.

——. *The Autobiography of Mark Twain.* Ed. Charles Neider. New York: Harper & Row, 1959.

——. "A Couple of Sad Experiences." *Galaxy,* 9 (1870), 858–61.

——. *Mark Twain in Eruption: Hitherto Unpublished Pages About Men and Events.* Ed. Bernard DeVoto. 1922; rpt. New York: Harper & Brothers, 1940.

——. *Mark Twain to Mrs. Fairbanks.* Ed. Dixon Wecter. San Marino, Calif.: Huntington Library, 1949.

————. *Mark Twain's Autobiography*. Ed. Albert Bigelow Paine. New York: Harper & Brothers, 1924.

————. *Mark Twain's (Burlesque) Autobiography and First Romance*. 1871; rpt. New York: Haskell House, 1970.

————. *Mark Twain's Letters from Hawaii*. Ed. A. Grove Day. New York: Appleton-Century, 1966.

————. *Mark Twain's Notebooks & Journals*. Vol. I, ed. Frederick Anderson et al. Berkeley: Univ. of California Press, 1975.

————. *Selected Mark Twain-Howells Letters, 1872–1910*. Ed. Frederick Anderson, William M. Gibson, and Henry Nash Smith. New York: Atheneum, 1968.

————. *Selected Shorter Writings of Mark Twain*. Ed. Walter Blair. Boston: Houghton Mifflin, 1962.

————. *The Works of Mark Twain*. Series Editor Frederick Anderson. Published for the Iowa Center for Textual Studies. Berkeley: Univ. of California Press.

Cohen, Hennig, and William B. Dillingham, eds. *Humour of the Old Southwest*. Boston: Houghton Mifflin, 1964.

Crockett, David. *A Narrative of the Life of David Crockett of the State of Tennessee*. Rpt. ed. and intro. James A. Shackford and Stanley J. Folmsbee. 1843; facsimile rpt. Knoxville: Univ. of Tennessee Press, 1973.

————. *Sketches and Eccentricities of Col. David Crockett of West Tennessee*. New York: J.&J. Harper, 1833.

Crockett Almanacs.

Crockett Almanac. Boston: Fisher and Brother, 1852.

Crockett's Almanac. Boston: Fisher and Brother, 1850.

Davy Crockett's Almanac. Boston: James Fisher, 1844, 1845.

Fisher's Crockett Almanac. New York and Philadelphia: Turner and Fisher, 1843.

Faulkner, William. *The Hamlet*. 1931; rpt. New York: Random House, 1964.

Franklin, Benjamin. *Benjamin Franklin's Letters to the Press, 1758–1775*. Ed. Verner W. Crane. Chapel Hill: Univ. of North Carolina Press, 1950.

Gerstacker, Friedrich. *Western Lands and Western Waters*. London: S.O. Beeton, 1864.

————. *Wild Sports in the Far West*. Boston: Crosby, Nichols & Co., 1859.

Haliburton, Thomas Chandler, ed. *The Americans at Home; or Byeways, Backwoods, and Prairies*. 2 vols. London: Hurst & Blackett, 1854.

————, ed. *Traits of American Humor, by Native Authors*. 3 vols. London: Colburn and Co., 1852.

Hall, James. *Letters from the West: Containing Sketches of Scenery, Manners, and Customs; and Anecdotes Connected with the First Settlements of the*

Western Sections of the United States. Intro. John T. Flanagan. 1828; rpt. Gainesville, Fla.: Scholars' Facsimiles & Reprints, 1967.

Harris, George W. *High Times and Hard Times*. Ed. Thomas Inge. Nashville, Tenn.: Vanderbilt Univ. Press, 1967.

————. *Sut Lovingood. Yarns Spun by a "Nat'ral Born Durn'd Fool." Warped and Wove for Public Wear*. New York: Fitzgerald Publishing Corporation, 1867.

Heller, Joseph. *Catch-22*. New York: Simon & Schuster, 1961.

Hurston, Zora Neale. *Mules and Men*. New York: Negro Univ. Press 1969.

Keillor, Garrison. *Lake Wobegon Days*. New York: Viking, 1985.

Lardner, Ring. *The Portable Ring Lardner*. Ed. Gilbert Seldes. New York: Viking Press, 1946.

Longstreet, Augustus Baldwin. *Georgia Scenes: Characters, Incidents, &c, in the First Half Century of the Republic by a Native Georgian*. 2nd ed. New York: Harper, 1840.

Meine, Franklin Julius, ed. *Tall Tales of the Southwest: An Anthology of Southern and Southwestern Humor, 1830–1860*. New York: Knopf, 1930.

Nye, Bill. *Forty Liars and Other Lies*. Chicago: Belford Clarke & Co., 1883.

Paulding, James Kirke. *The Lion of the West*. Rev. John Augustus Stone and William Bayle Bernard, ed. James N. Tidwell. Stanford, Calif.: Stanford Univ. Press, 1954.

Plutarch. *Moralia*. Trans. Frank Cole Babbitt. Vol. I. 1927; rpt. Cambridge, Mass.: Harvard Univ. Press, 1949.

Porter, William Sydney (O. Henry). *The Gentle Grafter*. 1904; rpt. New York: Doubleday, Page, 1916.

Porter, William T., ed. *The Big Bear of Arkansas, and Other Tales*. Philadelphia, 1843; facsimile rpt. New York: AMS Press, 1973.

————, ed. *A Quarter Race in Kentucky and Other Sketches, Illustrative of Scenes, Characters, and Incidents, Throughout "The Universal Yankee Nation."* Philadelphia: Carey and Hart, 1847.

Raspe, R.E., et al. *Singular Travels, Campaigns, and Adventures of Baron Münchausen*. Ed. and intro. John Carswell. 1948; rpt. New York: Dover, 1960.

Roth, Philip. *The Great American Novel*. New York: Holt, Rinehart and Winston, 1973.

————. *Portnoy's Complaint*. New York: Random House, 1967.

Shephard, Esther. *Paul Bunyan*. New York: Harcourt, Brace, 1924.

Schultz, Christian. *Travels on an Inland Voyage through the Territories of Indiana, Louisiana, Mississippi and New Orleans, Performed in the Years 1807 and 1808*. 1810; facsimile rpt. University Microfilms, 1979.

Spirit of the Times: A Chronicle of the Turf, Field Sports, Literature and the Stage. New York, 1831–1861.

Stevens, James. *Paul Bunyan*. Garden City, N.Y.: Garden City Publishing Co., 1925.

Taliaferro, Harden E. *Fisher's River Scenes and Characters*. New York: Harper & Brothers, 1859.

Wister, Owen. *The Virginian: A Horseman of the Plains*. New York: Macmillan, 1929.

Secondary Sources

Folklore

Aarne, Antii. *The Types of the Folktale; a Classification and Bibliography*. Trans. and enlarged by Stith Thompson. 1928; 2nd rev. ed. F.F. Communications, No. 3, Helsinki: Suomalainen Tiedeakatemia, 1964.

Abrahams, Roger D. "Folklore and Literature as Performance." *Journal of the Folklore Institute*, 9 (1972), 75–94.

———."Introductory Remarks to a Rhetorical Theory of Folklore."*Journal of American Folklore*, 81 (1968), 143–58.

Ball, John. "Style in the Folktale." *Folklore*, 65 (1954), 170–72.

Barnes, Daniel R. "Toward the Establishment of Principles for the Study of Folklore and Literature." *Southern Folklore Quarterly*, 43 (1979), 5–16.

Bascom, William. "The Forms of Folklore: Prose Narratives." *Journal of American Folklore*, 78 (1965), 3–20.

Baughman, Ernest W. *Type and Motif-Index of the Folktales of England and North America*. Bloomington: Indiana Folklore Series No. 20, 1966.

Bauman, Richard. "'Any Man Who Keeps More'n One Hound'll Lie to You': Dog Trading and Storytelling at Canton, Texas." In *"And Other Neighborly Names": Social Process and Cultural Image in Texas Folklore*. Ed. Richard Bauman and Roger D. Abrahams. Austin: Univ. of Texas Press, 1981, pp. 79–103.

Bauman, Richard, and Joel Sherzer, eds. *Explorations in the Ethnography of Speaking*. New York: Cambridge Univ. Press, 1974.

Beckham, Stephen Dow, ed. *Tall Tales from Rogue River: The Yarns of Hathaway Jones*. Bloomington: Indiana Univ. Press, 1974.

Ben-Amos, Dan. "Toward a Definition of Folklore in Context," In *Toward New Perspectives in Folklore*, ed. Americo Paredes and Richard Bauman. Publications of the American Folklore Society, Austin: Univ. of Texas Press, 1972.

Biebuyck-Goetz, Brunhilde. "'This is the Dyin' Truth': Mechanisms of Lying." *Journal of the Folklore Institute*, 14 (1977), 73–95.

Boatright, Mody C. *Folk Laughter on the American Frontier.* 1942; rpt. New York: Macmillan, 1949.

———. *Gib Morgan, Minstrel of the Oil Fields.* El Paso: Texas Folklore Society, 1945.

———. "The Tall Tale in Texas." *The South Atlantic Quarterly*, 30 (1931), 271–79.

Brunvand, Jan Harold. "Len Henry: North Idaho Munchausen." *Northwest Folklore*, 1 (1965), 11–19.

———. *The Study of American Folklore.* New York: Norton, 1968.

Cothran, Kay Lorraine. "Such Stuff as Dreams: A Folkloristic Sociology of Fantasy in the Okefenokee Rim, Georgia." Diss. Univ. of Pennsylvania, 1972.

———. "Talking Trash in the Okefenokee Swamp Rim, Georgia." *Journal of American Folklore*, 87 (1974), 340–56.

———. "Women's Tall Tales: A Problem in the Social Structure of Fantasy."*St. Andrews Review*, 2 (1972), 21–27.

Davidson, Bill. *Tall Tales They Tell in the Services.* New York: Crowell, 1943.

Degh, Linda. "Folk Narrative." In *Folklore and Folklife, An Introduction.* Ed. Richard M. Dorson. Chicago: Univ. of Chicago Press, 1972, 53–83.

Dondore, Dorothy. "Big Talk! The Flyting, the Bage, and the Frontier Boast." *American Speech*, 6 (1930), 45–55.

Dorson, Richard M. *Folklore and Fakelore: Essays Toward a Discipline of Folk Studies.* Cambridge, Mass.: Harvard Univ. Press, 1976.

———. *Jonathan Draws the Long Bow.* Cambridge, Mass.: Harvard Univ. Press, 1946.

———. "The Jonny-Cake Papers." *Journal of American Folklore*, 58 (1945).

———. *Man and Beast in American Comic Legend.* Bloomington: Indiana Univ. Press, 1982.

———. "Two City Yarnfests." *California Folklore Quarterly*, 5 (1946). 72–82.

Dundes, Alan. "The Study of Folklore in Literature and Culture." *Journal of American Folklore.* 78 (1965), 136–42.

———. "Texture, Text, and Context." *Southern Folklore Quarterly*, 28 (1964), 251–65.

Dundes, Alan, and Roger Abrahams. "On Elephantacy and Elephanticide." In *Analytic Essays in Folklore.* The Hague: Mouton, 1975.

Emrich, Duncan. *Folklore on the American Land.* Boston: Little, Brown, 1972.

Fowke, Edith. "In Defense of Paul Bunyan." *New York Folklore*, 5 (1979), 43–51.

Georges, Robert. "Towards an Understanding of Storytelling Events." *Journal of American Folklore*, 82 (1969), 313–28.

Halpert, Herbert. "John Darling, a New York Munchausen." *Journal of American Folklore*, 57 (1944), 97–106.

———. "Tall Tales and Other Yarns from Calgary, Alberta."*California Folklore Quarterly*, 4 (1945), 29–49.

Hennigsen, Gustav. "The Art of Perpendicular Lying, Concerning a Commercial Collecting of Norwegian Sailors' Tall Tales." Trans. Warren E. Roberts. *Journal of the Folklore Institute*, 2 (1965), 180–219.

Hymes, Dell. "Models of the Interaction of Language and Social Life." In *Directions in Sociolinguistics*. Ed. John J. Gumperz and Dell Hymes. New York: Holt, Rinehart and Winston, 1972.

Jansen, William Hugh. *Abraham "Oregon" Smith: Pioneer, Folk Hero, and Tale-Teller*. New York: Arno Press, 1977.

Joines, Jerry D. "Twelve Tall Tales From Wilkes Country." *North Carolina Folklore*, 20 (1972), 3–10.

Jones, Steven Swann. *Folklore and Literature in the United States*. New York: Garland, 1984.

Labov, William, and Joshua Waletzky. "Narrative Analysis: Oral Versions of Personal Experience." In *Essays on the Verbal and Visual Arts*. Ed. June Helm. Seattle: Proceedings of the 1966 Annual Spring Meeting of the American Ethnological Society, 1966.

Loomis, C. Grant. "The American Tall Tale and the Miraculous." *California Folklore Quarterly*, 4 (1945), 109–28.

———. "A Tall Tale Miscellany." *Western Folklore*, 6 (1947), 28–41.

Lunt, Richard K. "Jones Tracy: Tall Tale Hero from Mount Desert Island." *Northeast Folklore*, 10 (1968).

Masterson, James R. *Tall Tales of Arkansaw*. Boston: Chapman & Grimes, 1942.

McKeithan, D.M. "Bull Rides Described by 'Scroggins,' G.W. Harris, and Mark Twain." *Southern Folklore Quarterly*, 17 (1953), 241–43.

Mullen, Patrick B. *I Heard the Old Fisherman Say: Folklore of the Texas Gulf Coast*. Austin: Univ. of Texas Press, 1978.

Mullin, Susan. "Oregon's Huckleberry Finn: A Munchausen Enters Tradition." *Northwest Folklore*, 2 (1967), 19–25.

Paredes, Americo, and Richard Bauman, eds. *Toward New Perspectives in Folklore*. Austin: Univ. of Texas Press, 1972.

Propp, Vladimir. *Morphology of the Folktale*. Trans. Laurence Scott. *International Journal of American Linguistics*, 24. Bloomington: Indiana Univ. Research Center in Anthropology, Folklore, and Linguistics, 1958.

Randolph, Vance. *We Always Lie to Strangers: Tall Tales from the Ozarks*. New York: Columbia Univ. Press, 1951.

Rourke, Constance. "Paul Bunyan." *New Republic*, 23 (1920), 176–79.

Stahl, Sandra K.D. "Studying Folklore in American Literature." In *Handbook of American Folklore*, ed. Richard M. Dorson. Bloomington: Indiana Univ. Press, 1983.

———. "Style in Oral and Written Narrative." *Southern Folklore Quarterly*, 43 (1979), 39–62.

――――. "The Personal Narrative as Folklore." *Journal of the Folklore Institute*, 14 (1977), 9–30.

Stanley, David H. "The Personal Narrative and the Personal Novel: Folklore as Frame and Structure for Literature." *Southern Folklore Quarterly*, 43 (1979), 107–20.

Studer, Norman. "Yarns of a Catskill Woodsman." *New York Folklore Quarterly*, 11 (1955), 183–92.

Thomas, Gerald. *The Tall Tale and Philippe d'Alcripe: An Analysis of the Tall Tale Genre with Particular Reference to Philippe d'Alcripe's "La Nouvelle Fabrique des Excellents Traits de Verité," Together with an Annotated Translation of the Work*. Memorial Univ. of Newfoundland Folklore and Language Publication Series, no. 1; Bibliographic and Special Series, vol. 29. St. John's, Newfoundland: Memorial Univ. of Newfoundland, 1977.

Thompson, Stith. *The Folktale*. 1946; rpt. Berkeley: Univ. of California Press, 1977.

Toelken, Barre. *The Dynamics of Folklore*. Boston: Houghton Mifflin, 1979.

Welsch, Roger. *Catfish at the Pump: Humor and the Frontier*. Lincoln: Plains Heritage, 1982.

――――. *Shingling the Fog and Other Plains Lies*. Chicago: Swallow Press, 1972.

Wyatt, P.J. "So-Called Tall Tales about Kansas." *Western Folklore*, 22 (1963), 107–11.

Biography, Criticism, and the Psychology of Humor

Bakhtin, Mikhail. *Rabelais and His World*. Trans. Helene Iswolsky. Cambridge, Mass.: MIT Press, 1968.

Beidler, Philip D. "Realistic Style and the Problem of Context in *The Innocents Abroad* and *Roughing It*." *American Literature*, 52 (1980), 33–49.

Blair, Walter. *Horse Sense in American Humor From Benjamin Franklin to Ogden Nash*. Chicago: Univ. of Chicago Press, 1942.

――――. *Native American Humor*. 1937; rpt. New York: Chandler, 1960.

――――. "The Popularity of Nineteenth-Century American Humorists." *American Literature*, 3 (1931), 175–94.

――――. *Tall Tale America*. New York: Coward-McCann, 1944.

Blair, Walter, and Hamlin Hill. *America's Humor*. New York: Oxford Press, 1978.

Blair, Walter, and Franklin J. Meine. *Half Horse Half Alligator: The Growth of the Mike Fink Legend*. Chicago: Univ. of Chicago Press, 1956.

Boulding, Kenneth E. *The Image: Knowledge in Life and Society*. Ann Arbor: Univ. of Michigan Press, 1956.

Branch, Edgar Marquess. *The Literary Apprenticeship of Mark Twain; With Selections from His Apprentice Writing.* New York: Russell & Russell, 1966.

Bridgman, Richard. *The Colloquial Style in America.* New York: Oxford Univ. Press, 1966.

Brooks, Van Wyck. "Mark Twain's Humor." In *Mark Twain: A Collection of Critical Essays.* Ed. Henry Nash Smith. Englewood Cliffs, N.J.: Prentice-Hall, 1963.

Budd, Louis J. *Our Mark Twain: The Making of a Public Personality.* Philadelphia: Univ. of Pennsylvania Press, 1983.

Burke, Kenneth. "Literature as Equipment for Living." In *The Philosophy of Literary Form: Studies in Symbolic Action.* 1941; rpt. Baton Rouge: Louisiana State Univ. Press, 1967.

Caesar, Gene. *King of the Mountain Men: The Life of Jim Bridger.* New York: Dutton, 1961.

Cawelti, John G. *The Six-Gun Mystique.* Bowling Green, Ohio: Bowling Green Univ. Popular Press, 1984.

Chittenden, Hiram. *The Yellowstone National Park: Historical and Descriptive.* Cincinnati, 1895; rpt. Norman: Univ. of Oklahoma Press, 1964.

Covici, Pascal. *Mark Twain's Humor: The Image of a World.* Dallas: Southern Methodist Univ. Press, 1962.

Cox, James M. "Humor and America: The Southwestern Bear Hunt, Mrs. Stowe, and Mark Twain." *The Sewanee Review,* 83 (1975), 573–601.

———. *Mark Twain: The Fate of Humor.* Princeton, N.J.: Princeton Univ. Press, 1966.

Cox, S.S. "American Humor." *Harper's Magazine,* 80 (1875), 690–702, 847–59.

Day, Donald. "The Humorous Works of George Washington Harris." *American Literature,* 14 (1943), 391–406.

———. "The Life of George Washington Harris." *Tennessee Historical Quarterly,* 6 (1947), 3–38.

Dorson, Richard M. *Davy Crockett, American Comic Legend.* New York: Rockland Editions, 1939.

———. "The Identification of Folklore in American Literature." *Journal of American Folklore,* 70 (1957), 1–8.

Eastman, Max. "Humor and America." *Scribner's,* 100 (1936), 9–13.

Fender, Stephen. "'The Prodigal in a Far Country of Chawing Husks': Mark Twain's Search for a Style in the West." *Modern Language Review,* 71 (1976), 737–56.

Ferguson, DeLancey. "The Petrified Truth." *The Colophon,* 2 (1937), 189–96.

———. "The Roots of American Humor." *The American Scholar,* 4 (1935), 41–49.

Freud, Sigmund. "Jokes and the Comic." In *Comedy: Meaning and Form.* Ed. Robert W. Corrigan. Scranton, Pa.: Chandler, 1965.

Frye, Northrop. *Anatomy of Criticism: Four Essays.* Princeton, N.J.: Princeton Univ. Press, 1957.

Gorn, Elliot. "'Gouge and Bite, Pull Hair and Scratch': The Social Significance of Fighting in the Southern Backcountry." *American Historical Review,* 90 (1985), 18–43.

Greig, J.Y.T. *The Psychology of Laughter and Comedy.* 1923; rpt. New York: Cooper Square, 1969.

Gurewitch, Morton L. *Comedy: The Irrational Vision.* Ithaca: Cornell Univ. Press, 1975.

Harpham, Geoffrey Galt. *On the Grotesque: Strategies of Contradiction in Art and Literature.* Princeton, N.J.: Princeton Univ. Press, 1982.

Hauck, Richard Boyd. *A Cheerful Nihilism: Confidence and "The Absurd" in American Humorous Fiction.* Bloomington: Indiana Univ. Press, 1971.

Hill, Hamlin. *Mark Twain: God's Fool.* New York: Harper & Row, 1973.

Hedges, William L. *Washington Irving: An American Study, 1802–1832.* Goucher College Series. Baltimore: Johns Hopkins Press, 1965.

Hirsch, E.D. *The Philosophy of Composition.* Chicago: Univ. of Chicago Press, 1977.

Hoffman, Daniel G. *Form and Fable in American Fiction.* 1961: rpt. Norton, 1973.

————. *Paul Bunyan, Last of the Frontier Demigods.* Philadelphia, 1952; rpt. New York: Columbia Univ. Press, 1966.

Howard, Alan. "Huck Finn in the House of Usher: The Comic and Grotesque Worlds of *The Hamlet.*" *Southern Review,* 5 (1972), 125–46.

Howells, William Dean. "Mark Twain: An Inquiry." In *My Mark Twain.* Ed. Marilyn Austin Baldwin. Baton Rouge: Louisiana State Univ. Press, 1967, pp. 143–62.

Inge, M. Thomas, ed. *The Frontier Humorists: Critical Views.* Hamden, Conn.: Archon Books, 1975.

Iser, Wolfgang. *The Implied Reader: Patterns of Communication in Prose Fiction from Bunyan to Beckett.* 1972; rpt. Baltimore: Johns Hopkins Univ. Press, 1974.

————. "The Reality of Fiction: A Functionalist Approach to Literature." *New Literary History,* 7 (1976), 7–38.

Kaplan, Justin. *Mr. Clemens and Mark Twain: A Biography.* New York: Simon and Schuster, 1966.

Kazin, Alfred. *Bright Book of Life: American Novelists and Storytellers from Hemingway to Mailer.* 1971; rpt. Notre Dame: Univ. of Notre Dame Press, 1980.

Kenney, W. Howland, ed. *Laughter in the Wilderness: Early American Humor to 1783.* Kent, Ohio: Kent State Univ. Press, 1976.

Lemay, Leo. "The Text, Tradition and Themes of 'The Big Bear of Arkansas.'" *American Literature*, 47 (1975), 321–42.

Lillard, Richard G. "Contemporary Reaction to 'The Empire City Massacre.'" *American Literature*, 16 (1944), 198–203.

———. "Dan DeQuille, Comstock Reporter and Humorist." *The Pacific Historical Review*, 13 (1944), 251–59.

Loomis, C. Grant. "Hart's Tall Tales from Nevada. " *California Folklore Quarterly*, 4 (1945), 216–38, 351–58.

———. "The Tall Tales of Dan DeQuille." *California Folklore Quarterly*, 5 (1946), 26–71.

Lorch, Fred W. *The Trouble Begins at Eight: Mark Twain's Lecture Tours.* Ames: Iowa State Univ. Press, 1968.

Lynn, Kenneth S. *Mark Twain and Southwest Humor.* Boston: Little, Brown, 1959.

McClary, Ben Harris. "The Real Sut." *American Literature*, 27 (1955), 105–106.

Michelson, Bruce. "Mark Twain the Tourist: The Form of *The Innocents Abroad.*" *American Literature*, 49 (1977), 385–98.

Micklus, Robert. "Sut's Travels with Dad." *Studies in American Humor*, 1, New Series (1982), 89–101.

Miles, Elton. *Southwest Humorists.* Southwest Writers Series, 26. Austin: Steck-Vaughn, 1969.

Neal, John. "Story Telling." *New York Mirror*, 16 (1839).

Ong, Walter J., S.J. "The Writer's Audience is Always a Fiction." *PMLA*, 90 (1975), 9–21.

Paine, Albert Bigelow. *Mark Twain: A Biography.* 4 vols. New York: Harper, 1912.

Penrod, James. "Folk Humor in *Sut Lovingood's Yarns.*" *Tennessee Folklore Society Bulletin*, 16 (1950), 76–84.

Poe, Edgar A. Review of *Georgia Scenes. Southern Literary Messenger*, 2 (1836), 287–92.

Polk, Noel. "The Blind Bull, Human Nature: Sut Lovingood and the Damned Human Race." In *Gyascutus: Studies in Antebellum Southern Humorous and Sporting Writing.* Ed. James L.W. West III. *Costerus: Essays in English and American Language and Literature, New Series*, Vols. V–VI. Atlantic Highlands, N.J.: Humanities Press, 1978, pp. 13–49.

Rickels, Milton. *George Washington Harris.* New York: Twayne Publishers, 1965.

———. "The Grotesque Body of Southwestern Humor." In *Critical Essays on American Humor.* Ed. W. Bedford Clark and W. Craig Turner. Boston: G.K. Hall, 1984.

———. *Thomas Bangs Thorpe, Humorist of the Old Southwest.* Baton Rouge: Louisiana State Univ. Press, 1962.

Roth, Philip. "Reading Myself." *Partisan Review*, 40 (1973), 404–17.

Rourke, Constance. *American Humor: A Study of the National Character.*
 1931; rpt. New York: Harcourt, Brace, Jovanovich, 1959.

Rubin, Louis D., ed. *The Comic Imagination in American Literature.* New
 Brunswick, N.J.: Rutgers Univ. Press, 1973.

Ryle, Gilbert. *The Concept of Mind.* New York: Barnes & Noble [1950?].

Saum, Lewis O. *The Popular Mood of Pre-Civil War America.* Contributions
 in American Studies, 46. Westport, Conn.: Greenwood Press, 1980.

Schmitz, Neil. *Of Huck and Alice: Humorous Writing in American Literature.*
 Minneapolis: Univ. of Minnesota Press, 1983.

———. "Tall Tale, Tall Talk: Pursuing the Lie in Jacksonian Literature." *American Literature*, 48 (1977), 471–91.

Scholes, Robert. *Structuralism in Literature.* New Haven: Yale Univ. Press, 1974.

Scholes, Robert, and Robert Kellogg. *The Nature of Narrative.* New York: Oxford Univ. Press, 1966.

Slatoff, Walter. *With Respect to Readers: Dimensions of Literary Response.*
 Ithaca: Cornell Univ. Press, 1970.

Smith, Henry Nash. *Mark Twain: The Development of a Writer.* 1962; rpt. New
 York: Atheneum, 1972.

Tomkins, Jane, ed. *Reader-Response Criticism: From Formalism to Post-
 Structuralism.* Baltimore: Johns Hopkins Univ. Press, 1980.

Thompson, Harold W., and Henry Seidel Canby. "Humor." In *Literary History
 of the United States.* Ed. Robert E. Spiller et al. Rev. Ed. New York: Macmillan, 1957, p. 728.

Turner, Arlin. "Seeds of Literary Revolt in the Humor of the Old Southwest."
 Louisiana Historical Quarterly, 39 (1956), 143–51.

Wade, John Donald. *Augustus Baldwin Longstreet: A Study of the Development of Culture in the South.* New York, Macmillan, 1924.

Welsford, Enid. *The Fool: His Social and Literary History.* London: Faber and
 Faber, 1935.

Wilson, Edmund. *Patriotic Gore: Studies in the Literature of the American
 Civil War.* New York: Oxford Univ. Press, 1962.

Yates, Norris Wilson. *The American Humorist: Conscience of the Twentieth
 Century.* Ames: Iowa State Univ. Press, 1964.

———. *William T. Porter and the Spirit of the Times; a Study of the Big Bear
 School of Humor.* Baton Rouge: Louisiana State Univ. Press, 1957.

Index

The Tall Tale was designed by Sheila Hart; composed by Lithocraft, Inc., Grundy Center, Iowa; printed by Thomson-Shore, Inc., and bound by John H. Dekker & Sons, Grand Rapids, Michigan. The book was set in 10/12 Garamond with Garamond display and printed on 60-lb. Glatfelter.

THE UNIVERSITY OF TENNESSEE PRESS

KNOXVILLE 37996-0325